The Wondering Jew

My Journey into Judaism

Ellen Brazer

The Wondering Jew
My Journey into Judaism

For information go to:
www.ellenbrazer.com
or write to the author at
ellenb9815@bellsouth.net

ISBN: 978-0-692-73994-5

Cover Art Designed by Barbara Glicken

Printed in the United States of America

Other books written by Ellen Brazer

Clouds Across the Sun
And So It Was Written

This book is dedicated to my husband Mel Brazer.
You are the light and the breath of my life.
I will love you forever and a day!

I have written this book to honor the
blessed memory of my parents:
Esther and Irving Glicken

TABLE OF CONTENTS

Glossary

Aron Ha'Kodesh: Ark that that holds the Torah in a synagogue.

Ashkenazi: Jew of central or eastern European descent.

Bar Mitzvah: Religious initiation ceremony of a Jewish boy at the age of thirteen.

Challah: White leavened bread typically plaited and baked to celebrate the Sabbath.

Chametz: Food mixed with leaven and prohibited on Passover.

Chasidim: An Orthodox adherent of Hasidism.

Chutzpah: Shameless audacity and impudence.

Dreidel: A small four-sided spinning top with a Hebrew letter on each side.

Eretz Yisrael: The land of Israel.

Etrog: A yellow citrus fruit used for the holiday of Sukkot as one of the four spices.

Gantseh megillah: Big deal!

Gilgul: The Kabbalistic concept of reincarnation. Hebrew: cycle or wheel.

Haggadah: Text recited on the first two nights of Passover.

Hamantashen: A small triangular cake filled with poppy seeds, honey or prunes for the holiday of Purim.

Haredim: Orthodox Jews who reject modern secular culture.

Ha'Shem: G-d.

Kabbalah: Ancient Jewish mystical interpretation of the Hebrew Bible.

Kaddish: A Jewish liturgical prayer recited by mourners. Also regularly recited in the synagogue service.

Kiddush: The blessing over the wine.

Klutz: An awkward, clumsy person who drops things.

Kugel: A sweet noodle or potato pudding.

Kvetch: A person who complains a great deal.

L'shanah Tovah: A good year.

Lulav: Frond of a date palm used during Sukkot.

Mazel tov: Said to wish someone congratulations or good luck.

Megillot: The five scrolls that are part of the Writings in the Hebrew Bible.

Menorah: The sacred seven-branched candelabrum used in the Temple in Jerusalem. Also, with nine branches, used during Chanukah.

Midrash: Ancient commentary; stories.

Minyan: A quorum of ten men (or in some synagogues men and women) over the age of 13 required for traditional Jewish public worship.

Misheberach: A prayer for healing.

Mishnah: Collection of material embodying the oral tradition of Jewish law and forming the first part of the Talmud.

Mishneh Torah: The code of Jewish law authored by Maimonides.

Nazarite: An Israelite consecrated to the service of G-d.

Oy Gevalt: Yiddish phrase of exclamation, surprise, or incredulity.

Oy Vey: Dismay or grief.

Parsha: Any of the sections of the Torah read in synagogue.

Payot: Hebrew for side locks of side curls worn by Orthodox men.

Pitam: The extension that grows from the Etrog.

Sanhedrin: The assembly or council of men appointed to exercise authority in the Land of Israel in ancient times.

Schlep: To carry or pull with difficulty.

Schnaps: Whiskey.

Sephardic: Descendants of Jews from Spain and Portugal.

Shabbas/Shabbat: The Jewish Sabbath from Sundown Friday night until Sundown Saturday night.

Shamus candle: The ninth candle (servant candle) used to light the other candles for the Chanukah menorah.

Shanda: A shame; scandal.

Sheket B'vakasha: Hebrew for "Quiet please."

Shema: Hear, O Israel, the centerpiece of prayer for morning and evening prayers.

Shiva: A period of seven-days formal mourning for the dead.

Shofar: A ram's horn used as a trumpet for specific Jewish holidays.

Siddur: The Jewish prayer book.

Sukkah: A temporary shelter used for meals during the holiday of Succoth.

Tallit: A fringed prayer shawl.

Talmud: A book of commentary on Jewish civil and ceremonial law.

Tanakh: Acronym for the Five Books of Moses.

Tashlich: Symbolic casting off of sins by tossing pieces of bread into a flowing body of water on the holiday of Rosh Hashanah.

Tehillim: The book of Psalms.

Teffilin: Two small black boxes with black leather straps attached that are used in Jewish prayer.

Torah: The scroll containing the Five Book of Moses.

Tzimmes: A Jewish stew of sweetened vegetables or vegetables with fruit and or meat.

Yahrtzeit: The anniversary of a family member's death.

Yarmulke: A skullcap worn in public by Orthodox Jews and only in the synagogue by other less observant Jews.

Yizkor: A memorial service held by Jews on certain holy days for deceased relatives.

Zohar: The foundational work in literature of Jewish mystical thought known as Kabbalah.

Hebrew Months

Nissan	30 days	March-April
Lyar	29 days	April-May
Sivan	30 days	May-June
Tammuz	29 days	June-July
Av	30 days	July-August
Elul	29 days	August September
Tishri	30 days	September-October
Cheshvan	29 or 30 days	October-November
Kislev	29 days	November-December
Tevet	29 days	December-January
Shevat	30 days	January-February
Adar 1	(leap years) 30 days	February-March
Adar II (Adar Beit in leap years only)		February-March 13th month in leap years

ACKNOWLEDGMENTS

Writing is a solitary pursuit, until it isn't! To that end, I have many people to thank. This book was birthed because of my friend Michele Kabat who convinced me to pursue my dream and write a non-fiction book about Judaism. I owe a huge thank you to Maxine Cahn, my editor extraordinaire and my friend. You did it again! Your tireless commitment is always astounding.

Barbara Glicken, (married to my brother Howard) created my fabulous cover. She is my confidant and my friend for life. What more can I say? Love to Lily Prellezo and Orlando Rodriquez, my devoted writing group. They were there for me every step of the way. Dr. Anita Meinbach was my inspiration and a critical piece in the puzzle. Her intellect and ability to see beyond the obvious helped me bring this book to fruition. *The Wondering Jew* title was her fabulous idea!

Janet Wolk was my go to buddy for any questions I had about Judaism. She gave me great advice and listened for hours as I rambled on about the book. Thanks for reading and being my mentor. I am sending a very special thanks to Ruth Schlossman in Israel. When she read my first draft, Ruth had the courage to tell me the truth. She sent me back to the drawing board, saying: *let us feel what you felt*. I hope I did that Ruth. Dr. Diane Wander was one of my readers, and I thank her.

Whenever I got overwhelmed, I turned to my friends for a respite. My cousin and adopted sister Judi Wolowitz and her husband Charlie opened their home for many a weekend retreat. Always fun and laughter! Michele and Larry Kabat are the kindest people I have ever known. Marjorie (my best weekly lunch buddy) and Alan Goldberg, Miriam Matloff, (my friend forever) Dr. Susan and Gary Weiner (you light up our lives). Anita and Jay Meinbach, (new friends that we adore). Maxine and Sam Cahn, Barbara and Bob Roseff, Gail Newman and Bob Shlossman are all my life long friends. I am truly blessed.

Rabbi Marc Philippe of Temple Emanuel on Miami Beach has enriched my life in so many ways. Thank you from the bottom of my heart. I also want to express my appreciation to Rabbi Mann from the Chabad of the Venetian Islands. Your weekly classes have opened my mind and my heart.

The most important people in my life are my children and grandchildren. Mel and I have a combined family of six children, and I would never have a book published without naming every single one. I will begin with the children on my side:

Todd Brazer and his girls, Jordyn and Emma

Carrie Brazer and her boys, Max and Jacob

Judd Brazer (wife Ayda) and their girls Tiffany and Julia.

I hope you know you are everything to me!

On Mel's side, we have:

Barry and Ellen Brazer and their girls, Heidi (husband Jordan Tacktill) and their children, Dylan and Dean. Samantha (Husband Evan Rosenbaum) and their son Wesley

Mitchell and Becky Brazer and their children, Megan (husband Todd Cribbs) and Mathew (wife, Jessie).

Bonnie (husband Joe Grote) and their children, Rachel, Alexandria and Ryan.

Thank you for being my family.

By the way, the total is 30 and counting!

Chapter 1

THE DNA OF JUDAISM

This is my journey

I was a twice-a-year Jew: I attended synagogue on *Yom Kippur* and *Rosh Hashanah*. Out of a strong feeling of obligation we always belonged to a synagogue, mostly Reform. Because I love the Jewish traditions that connect us to our heritage, my sons became *Bar Mitzvah* and my daughter became *Bat Mitzvah*. I became *Bat Mitzvah* at thirty-eight.

Still, I was a Jew in name only until my husband and I traveled to Israel in 1985. The moment my feet first touched the ground of *Eretz Yisrael,* something shifted inside of me. Over the following days, the people of Israel became my people—the survivors of the Holocaust and all the others who had carved out a country from the swamps and the deserts, defeating all who dared challenge their right to exist. This was not about religion for me. It was about pride in my Jewish homeland and its people. That realization changed me dramatically and forever.

By the time we returned to Miami, I was an ardent Zionist determined to do whatever I could to insure that the State of Israel would remain forever secure. I committed myself to the Jewish Federation, joining every committee that would take me.

At home, to honor the six million Jews who died in the holocaust, I insisted that we celebrate Shabbat. My teenagers were not allowed to go out on Friday night before we lit the candles and had a Shabbat dinner. I can still see their incredulous faces and remember their remarks: *No big deal. This won't last. It's just one of Mom's weird obsessions.* They were partially wrong as we continued to have Shabbat dinners for a few years. And then they were right as well, the dinners just drifted out of our lives and I can't remember how or why.

Over the years, I have been involved and uninvolved in various aspects of Jewish life. One thing remained constant: my commitment to the State of Israel and her people.

Yet, regardless of where I was in my journey, I never found solace in the prayers or within the walls of a synagogue. Part of the reason was my ignorance. I studied the history of the Jews but never the religion. One of the big reasons: I did not like all the rules attached to being Jewish!

However, in recent years, certain life-changing events sent me on a journey of exploration, bringing me closer to Judaism than I ever imagined. I became "a wondering Jew."

Through the pages of this book, my intention is to describe what I discovered about Judaism through the camera of my life experiences. Let me add that throughout the book I will write the word G-d with a hyphen. The reason: Only when praying is G-d's name fully written.

After reflecting on the completed first draft of this book, I realized I did not accomplish my goals. Instead, I had avoided sharing my deepest thoughts and feelings about my relationship with Judaism.

I know this is due to my self-protective nature. I am more comfortable being distanced from the here and now—expressing myself through the fictional characters in my books. In fact, that is the reason I write historical fiction: It allows me to keep a protective buffer over my personal life.

And so, I began to revise. In doing so, I did my best to peel away the layers and take a look at where I am as a Jew and a person.

Dramatic events in my life led me *back* to Judaism. I say *back* because as Jews, none of us are ever really that far away. The fog may have set in, and we may have looked elsewhere for answers, but in the end, G-d willing, we begin to remember that we all stood together at Mt. Sinai and that Judaism is in our DNA.

CHAPTER 2

THE MOMENTS THAT CHANGE OUR LIVES

The afternoon in 2012, I was working with my writing group when the call came from my brother. He was worried that my father had not called to wish his wife, Barbara, a happy birthday. Barbara was one of my father's favorite people in the world. He would *never* not call!

Dad, at ninety-two, was a vivacious, thoughtful and gentle man who still drove at night and played a mean game of golf. He was the patriarch of our family, beloved and honored.

I had tried to reach him several times earlier in the day, but he had not answered. I thought he was out for a walk or doing errands from the running list he always kept.

The person who lived closest to my father's townhouse was my beloved former daughter-in-law, Randi, the mother of my two grand-daughters. I called Randi and pleaded, "Please, just drive over to Papa's house to see if his car is in the driveway." I could hear her fighting back the terror as she said, "Oh no! What will I do if it's there?"

Ten minutes later my cell phone rang. Randi was weeping. "The car is here." She adored my father, and I was and still am so sorry that I put her through the ordeal that ensued. Yet, there is not another person in the world who could have shown the dignity and grace that she displayed on that horrific day.

She stayed on the phone with me until the police arrived and broke in the door. From the moment they entered his two-story townhouse, they knew my father was dead. She stayed outside relating everything that was happening. I was forty-five minutes away! I knew I could not drive. I called my husband, making up an excuse for him to pick me up, without telling him what had happened. My father was my husband's best friend.

I believe we survived that ride to my father's house because G-d had given us a very special gift, one that few people talk about. That gift is bestowed upon us when something tragic happens in our lives. Some call it shock. I prefer to think of it as a protective shield that encapsulates our mind and body, allowing us to move, react and make decisions even though, we have become a shadow of our logical selves.

My brother and sister-in-law and my daughter were at the house when my husband and I arrived. When I walked up the stairs, my daughter, seven months pregnant, was alone in the room with my father. Daddy was on the floor in his boxer shorts. He had passed away as I hope I will—lying on the carpet doing exercises. My husband stayed a few minutes, and then he went downstairs.

I sat beside my father on the floor: staring, talking to him, touching him. With death, his sun-lined face was smooth. I noticed a Band-Aid on his big toe. I remembered him telling me his toe was sore. Had I asked why? I couldn't remember. I kept looking back at the Band-Aid. It seemed so absurd, so ridiculous: He was dead!

Some images remain forever. As I write this, the feelings of that moment are crashing in. My daughter Carrie and I just sat with him as we waited for the funeral home to retrieve his body.

Losing a second parent was different in ways I never expected. With my beloved mother Esther deceased for several years, the only person left in the world who would ever love me unconditionally was now gone.

Here I was at one of the darkest moments in my life, and yet, I felt sheathed in a gentled light. I could sense the presence of G-d. I could feel my father's soul hovering, whispering his love. I understood in words never spoken that he would always be with me just as my mother has always been with me. I would not trade those three hours that we sat with my father for anything. I now know, that day was the beginning of it all—not the end.

In closing this chapter, I want to share the words said by my seven-year-old granddaughter when she was told of my father's passing. Randi told her that Papa had died because his heart was tired, and it had broken. My little Emma replied: *But my heart was not ready for his heart to be broken.*

CHAPTER 3

IT ALL BEGAN WITH A PROMISE

Dad was a religious man. He went to the conservative synagogue every Saturday. He was blessed to have my brother and me, seven grandchildren and five great grandchildren. After services every Saturday, he would call each of us to wish us a *Shabbat Shalom,* never pushing his beliefs on any of us. When I would call him later in the day, on the Sabbath, and ask what he was doing, he would always say the same thing: "My *Shabbas* thing. I am reading and relaxing."

I can still envision my family sitting in a circle in the rabbi's study the day after my father passed away. As is the custom in Judaism, we took turns talking about him as the rabbi listened.

When it was my turn, I told the Rabbi that my father used to tease me, saying he wanted me to recite *Kaddish* for him when he died. *Kaddish* for a dead parent entails eleven months of going to synagogue every day to say a prayer that does not even mention death or the departed. It is a prayer of thanksgiving, praise of G-d and concludes with a prayer for peace.

I always replied to my father's request by insisting he was not going to die and then add, "Please don't lay that on me!" We would laugh.

When I told the Rabbi my father's request, I really expected him to reply, That's very nice. I think it would be lovely if you went every

Saturday. What I did not know was that the Conservative Movement had changed. Women were now counted in the *minyan*. A *minyan* is a quorum of ten Jews over the age of thirteen needed in order to recite the *Kaddish* blessing aloud. The rabbi looked at me and smiled. He said, "I think that it would be wonderful for you to fulfill your father's wishes."

Looking back, I know I would have fulfilled my father's wishes regardless of what the Rabbi might have said that day. In my heart, I had made a promise to my father, even if I never made that vow aloud. How could I not? My father had set a lifetime example for all of us, and I felt obligated to honor his commitment to Judaism.

Dad was sixteen years old when his father died leaving four children, a wife and no money. Dad was a teenager and a star basketball player in High School (1936), but he attended synagogue every day for the eleven months. He did the same a lifetime later when his mother died at the age of ninety-eight.

When my mother passed away in 2005, after a marriage of sixty plus years, my father said *Kaddish* yet again, even with his broken heart. At that time, I said the prayer everyday by myself in my home, just Mom, G-d and me. It was not that I loved my mother any less than I loved my father, it was just never even brought up: that I should go to synagogue to say *Kaddish* for my mother.

The commitment of saying *Kaddish* got Dad out of bed early each day. He made new friends: like-minded people who shared his faith and devotion. I believe it helped get him through that first year. I didn't know it at the time, but it would do the very same thing for me. The moment I made this commitment to myself, my life changed.

The Cuban Hebrew Congregation was the only conservative synagogue near my condominium on South Beach that had morning services. Services were at 7:30 AM. I remember that first day as if it were yesterday. First, I could not find a place to park. The doorway into the building is around the back, and I could not find my way in. By the time I figured it out, I was already late and crying. Swiping tears from my face, I finally found my way inside.

I had my father's *tallit*, prayer shawl, and his *yarmulke* with me in the frayed blue velvet bag he had used for over fifty years. I brought the *yarmulke* to my mouth to kiss it before putting in on my head. The little round gold embroidered head covering still smelled like my father. I could not believe it! I could sense him through his scent. As I sat down, I wrapped that *tallit* around my shoulders, feeling as though my father was hugging me.

Something magical was taking place, but it didn't last long. By the time I figured out what book to use and what page they were on, I was frantic—a stranger in a strange land. I had learned Hebrew twenty-five years earlier for my Bat Mitzvah, but the letters had drifted from my memory. The Hebrew looked so foreign, it might as well have been written in Chinese.

To make things worse, I did not know that on Monday and Thursday they read the *Torah*, which added a half hour to, what I considered, an already too-long service.

So now here I was beginning my sentence: to attend synagogue seven days a week for eleven months! When the *Torah* was carried down the aisle, I knew enough to use my prayer shawl to kiss the scroll. A man about my father's age, a man I later learned was named Rav Malka, began reading the designated weekly portion from the *Torah*. After he finished reading, the old rabbi turned to me.

"You are here to say *Kaddish*?"

I nodded.

"Come," he said, beckoning me forward. "What was your father's name?"

"Irving Glicken," I replied.

"What was his Hebrew name?"

I was horrified as I shook my head, and my eyes filled with tears. I didn't know.

"Shh. It's okay," he whispered. "You can find out. What is your Hebrew name?"

That one I knew, and I told him. Then he said a prayer over me, just words in Hebrew that I didn't understand. But those words swirled around me as if he were taking me into his arms.

It was now time to say the *Kaddish*. Rav Malka led me in prayer, saying each word slowly, allowing me to grieve. When I went back to my seat, I knew I was exactly where I was supposed to be.

CHAPTER 4

TEMPLE 101
OUR TEACHERS COME IN ALL
SHAPES, SIZES AND RELIGIONS

As far as I know, there is no definitive modern-day book that a layperson can read that says: Start on this page, then turn to that page, and you will learn how to be a Jew. The reason: Judaism is obscure and complicated, based on commentary, faith and stories—many of them fantastical.

Four years later, I am still taking baby steps, and I still have doubts and questions as I seek an understanding of Judaism. My biggest obstacle: the Holocaust. It seems to be that one impenetrable question that invades my thoughts whenever I read the daily prayers. I find myself asking: "Where was G-d during the Holocaust? Why didn't He stop Hitler? Why did He allow six million Jews to die?"

I tell myself, it was man not G-d, who allowed Hitler and the Nazis to rule. Then I recite the prayers, the vows that promise G-d will always protect his *Chosen People*. Doubt rears its ugly head, and I am back to square one—questioning my faith. Judaism teaches us that we do not have the capacity to understand G-d's decisions. For now, that is the only precept I fully understand and accept.

It took a while after my father's passing for me to go back to work on the first draft of my book, *And So It Was Written*. This historical novel is set in the second century of the Common Era. During that time, the renowned Rabbi Akiva declared a man named Shimon Bar Kokhba the Messiah of the Jewish people. Under the leadership of this false Messiah, the Jews defeated the Roman Empire and ruled Israel for three glorious years! If this is the first time you are hearing this, you are not alone.

Whenever I do a book talk and ask for a show of hands as to how many in the room have heard of Bar Kokhba—only a few hands are held up! Yet, in Israel the children learn about this great warrior in kindergarten.

There is no doubt in my mind why. Our rabbis see Bar Kokhba as an imposter, the false Messiah! They focus on the end result of our short-lived victory: the slaughter and exile of our people. I believe the Israelis focus on other aspects: Jews as warriors and Bar Kokhba as one of the world's great generals.

In my book, I build a fictional Third Temple. That came about during my initial research, when I learned of coins discovered that were used as currency during the Bar Kokhba era. One of the coins had a picture of a Temple that looked nothing like the First or Second Temple. It made no sense to me that the Jewish rulers of the time would use a different depiction for the Temple. Then I discovered a book written by a rabbi that put forth the premise that a Third Temple might have been built during those three years of Jewish rule.

The idea of writing a fictional account of a Third Temple had intrigued me from the very beginning. But as I began to rewrite, I realized that my words now felt hollow, like grains of sand sifting through my fingers. How could I write about a Third Temple when I knew nothing about the First or Second Temples? In my heart, I knew that I could spend years researching and still never touch on the true meaning of what the Temples meant to the Jewish people.

I decided to write to some universities looking for a Judaic scholar. I received a letter from a professor who told me that one of the great scholars of our time was in Miami at Florida International University. His name is Erik Larson (not the author). I called and made an appointment.

His office was small, a computer on the desk, his bicycle leaning against the wall. He was so young and handsome. I was certain I had the wrong room. I later learned that he spoke fourteen languages, one of them ancient Aramaic. More importantly, he was the youngest man to ever work on deciphering the Dead Sea Scrolls, brought to Israel by the rabbis. As unimaginable as it seemed, I was about to learn about Judaism from a non-Jew. And it would not be the first time. Two out of three other members of my writing group are Catholic, and they knew more about my Judaism than I did.

In a subsequent meeting, Dr. Larson put a rendering of the First and Second Temples on his computer screen. He told me to try and imagine what it must have been like for a farmer or a shepherd to enter Jerusalem and approach the largest edifice in the world. He was kind and patient as he walked me through the Temple, showing me where the women would have stood. He showed me the location of the *Aron Ha'Kodesh*, the place where the Ten Commandments were held, where the priests stood and where the sacrifices were made.

Sacrifices! The word and the idea mortified me. I think I can make this statement and be fairly accurate: Most Jews do not know how, why or in what manner sacrifices were made on the Temple Mount. You may feel like this is the last thing you needed to learn about Judaism, and you might be right. But it is fascinating.

Dr. Larson explained that tens of thousands gathered every day at the Temple. Here is a bit of information that really surprised me: As long as the Temple stood, Jews did not pray directly to G-d. We prayed through the priests, bringing our most prized and perfect animal to be offered as a sacrifice to G-d. The animal was slaughtered in the courtyard, north of the altar. After the animal's neck was cut with a perfect blade, causing instant death, a special vessel was used to receive blood from the animal's neck. The blood was then sprinkled in various areas of the Temple according to the laws regulating the designated offering.

The laws are complicated, and I will spare you the details. What is important is that I walked out of the professor's office that day empowered and ready to begin my rewrite of *And So It Was Written*.

I have come to believe that G-d has a plan for each of us. I see it as a complicated jigsaw puzzle. On our journey through life, we have to try and make the pieces fit. And just like a puzzle, sometimes we pick up the wrong piece.

Looking at life through this analogy, I have no doubt my father's request that I say *Kaddish* was one of the pieces in my puzzle. It brought me into the synagogue, into the Jewish world and led me to a deeper understanding of my heritage and myself. That dawning enlightenment was the reason I was able to finish *And So It Was Written*.

CHAPTER 5

ONE NEVER KNOWS

*A*nd So It Was Written is set in *Ein Gedi*, an oasis in the Negev Desert. The *Ein Gedi* that I saw in my imagination is purely fictional—although many passages in the biblical writings refer to the inhabitants of *Ein Gedi*. Today *Ein Gedi* is a glorious nature reserve.

In 2013, Rabbi Marc, the rabbi I prayed with every day from Temple Emmanuel on Miami Beach, went to Israel with his wife and three sons. Rabbi Marc Skyped from Israel to tell me he and his family were on their way to Masada when they passed a sign pointing to an excavation in *Ein Gedi*. "How could we not go?" he said to me.

His next words are etched in my memory. "Ellen, they have uncovered a synagogue. Not just a mosaic floor, but walls as well. And it looks exactly like the synagogue you described in your book!"

My heart pounded in my chest, and my breath stuttered. I got off the phone and said to my husband, "We have to go to Israel. I have to see that synagogue!"

Five months later, my husband and I were driving through the surrealistic wilderness of the Judean desert, on our way to *Ein Gedi*. The topography was both tranquil and fierce. Surrounded by mountains, the sky above was royal blue, the land varying hues of yellow, beige and gold.

Following the signs, I remember getting out of the car and thinking that it was not very impressive, this excavation I had come to see. There was a metal table set up, and on it were placed some brochures explaining what had been unearthed: an ancient synagogue from the second century.

I followed a path marked by stones and stood on trembling legs in that excavated synagogue. As I stood there, I expected to feel the earth shake beneath my feet and the sky to fill with lightning bolts. Tears sprung to my eyes. I felt nothing.

Yes, it was true: This synagogue looked like the one I had described in my book. But if this was my synagogue, then why did it feel so wrong? I wandered around touching the stone walls and breathing in the ancient musty sweet scent. I walked every inch, and that is when I discovered a small plaque stuck into a corner. It dated the building a hundred years after my story.

This was not the synagogue I had seen in my mind's eye. Still, I believe with all my heart that one day they will dig closer to the waterfall of *Ein Gedi*. When they do, they will find the city and the synagogue I saw in my imagination.

As we drove from *Ein Gedi*, I had so many opposing emotions. I was thrilled that excavations had begun, knowing that once the Israelis began to excavate, they would continue to do so. But I was so disappointed that this was not the synagogue I imagined. Part of me just wanted to go back to the hotel, take a long shower and cry in private. But we were only a short drive from Masada. And I would never visit Israel without visiting that majestic symbol of Judaism.

Masada sits atop a rock plateau in the Judean desert, overlooking the Dead Sea. Little did I know that the mystical experience I longed for would happen on Masada.

In 31 BCE, (before the common era) Herod the Great built a fabulous palatial palace as a retreat on the mountain fortress of Masada. Ninety-seven years later, the First Great Jewish Rebellion against Rome began. At that time, a group of Jewish zealots managed to overtake the Roman garrison holding Masada. When Jerusalem finally fell to the Romans and the Second Temple was destroyed, hundreds of zealots fled with their families from Jerusalem seeking refuge on Masada.

As inconceivable as it seems, the Jews managed to hold out against the Romans on Masada for three long years. Then in 73 CE, (common era) the Tenth Legion marched against the Jewish stronghold. A siege was implemented, and a wall was built. Using thousands of tons of stone and thousands of Jewish prisoners-of-war, a three hundred and seventy-five-foot rampart was constructed. In 74 CE, the mountain walls of Masada were breached.

Two women survived the attack and told their story to Josephus Flavius, governor of Galilee. His is the only written account we have of what took place on Masada. What follows is Flavius' account of what happened.

Elazar's final speech to his followers on Masada: *Since we long ago resolved never to be servants to the Romans, nor to any other than to G-d Himself, Who alone is the true and just LORD of mankind, the time is now come that obliges us to make that resolution true in practice ... We were the very first that revolted, and we are the last to fight against them; and I cannot but esteem it as a favor that G-d has granted us, that it is still in our power to die bravely, and in a state of freedom.*

Flavius, the historian's comments: *The defenders – almost one thousand men, women and children – led by Elazar ben Yair, burnt down* *the fortress and killed each other. The Zealots cast lots to choose ten men to kill the remainder. They then chose among themselves the one man who would kill the survivors. That last Jew then killed himself.*

In Jewish tradition, suicide is a sin. In the *Talmud*, the rabbinical interpretations of the *Torah* it says: *Against your will you were fashioned, and against your will you were born, and against your will you live, and against your will you die, and against your will you will hereafter have account and reckoning before the King of Kings, the Holy One, blessed be He"* (*Ethics of the Fathers* 4:29). Still, the Jews of Masada chose to die rather than be enslaved.

Masada stands as a symbol

It is mandatory for all young men and women to join the IDF, the Israeli Defense Forces, when they graduate high school. Many of these young soldiers choose to take their oath to protect the State of Israel while standing atop Masada. These young people know, in war, they are all that stands between survival and death, for not just themselves but for their families.

I will never forget the first time I visited Masada. There was a group of young Jewish teenagers from around the world. They spoke different languages, and yet they were standing together holding hands and singing Hebrew songs: all with the same melody and the same words. I wept, overcome with the joy of experiencing such a special moment.

CHAPTER 6

MIRACLE ON MASADA

As I walked around the fortress of Masada that day, I saw it with older eyes and a different perspective. Every rock and every step I took felt holy. There are nooks and crannies throughout the excavation. Entering one, I was surprised to see a scribe sitting at a table writing a *Torah* scroll. That surprise turned to wonder in seconds. What a glorious moment, watching the birth of a *Torah* scroll while standing on Masada!

Writing a *Torah* is a religious act, and the scribes who write them are specially trained rabbinical scholars. The *Torah* scrolls are written on parchment made from the skin of a kosher animal. Special ink is prepared, and only a quill, usually from a turkey feather, is used.

The pieces of parchments are sewn together with thread made from animal veins. The completed scroll is then attached to wooden rollers. No instrument made from iron or steel can be used in the creation of a *Torah* scroll: These metals are seen as instruments of war.

Every *Torah* scroll is an exact duplicate of every *Torah* that came before it! There are three hundred and four thousand, eight hundred and five hand-written letters in a *Torah*, and it takes approximately two thousand hours to complete a scroll. That translates to a full-time job for a year to create just one *Torah*. If a mistake is made when writing the scroll, then that entire portion must be rewritten.

It is said that the *Torah* was originally dictated from G-d to Moses, letter by letter. There is a *Midrash*, a story written to help interpret the *Torah*, that tells us: *Before his death, Moses wrote thirteen Torah Scrolls. Twelve of these were distributed to each of the twelve Tribes. The thirteenth was placed in the Ark of the Covenant along with the Tablets* (*Devarim Rabba* 9:4.)

Determined to take part in this mystical experience, I waited in line to have the scribe write a letter in the *Torah* for me. When it was my turn he said, "Make a prayer first." I closed my eyes, and I prayed.

"What did you pray for?" he asked, his voice gentle as a breeze.

"Peace," I replied.

He shook his head. "Everyone in the world should pray for peace. Today I want you to pray for yourself."

A bit stunned, I closed my eyes again. I remember thinking if I am going to pray for myself, then I am going to be really selfish.

"What did you pray for?" the rabbi asked again.

"I prayed that I would find the story for my next book."

At that moment, something magical happened as the rabbi captured me with his eyes. All sound evaporated. I could not feel my body. I was aware only of his presence.

"What do you write?" he asked.

"Jewish historical fiction," I replied.

The rabbi smiled as he put his hand in his pocket and pulled out a handful of shekels. "What you write is important and thousands will read your words." He placed the money in my hand. "Please send me your books."

I was crying. I said, "Rabbi, I don't want your money."

"If you do not take my money, then I cannot accept the books."

I sent the books the moment I got home. Certain that my life had shifted during that experience on Masada, I expected the writer's block I had been suffering through for months would be miraculously lifted. That was not to be the case.

I started four different books. Each time, I found myself cornered and unable to continue. It would be two long years before I came to what you are now reading.

What kept me from losing hope that my next book would be revealed to me was a letter that came months after I returned home from Israel. I have not corrected it. His words are just as they were written.

> *Dear Ellen, I read one of your books, "And So It Was Written" and was moved to tears. I must say that I should of held your book from the moment I started reading it, and not leave it until I'm finished, If only I could afford the time. I had to read sections in distant times like Shabbat Afternoon. So it became quite a routine part of my Shabbat. Along with my presence at Masada, I could almost see the characters of your book, hiding in the crevices of the rocks in the desert of Judea and Ein Gedi. I'm eager to read the second book, my wife gulped it in one week and enjoyed very much. Thank you. The book you wrote is really a gift to the people of Israel, so there is no doubt, You are some of the messiah breeze. May G-d bless your hands to continue to write books and bring a smile or emotional longing, on our way to a world of peace and love. With Love & Blessing,*
> *Rabbi Ariel Joshua Louis*

This letter is the reason I continue to write.

CHAPTER 7

HOME IS WHERE THE HEART IS

My life began in Binghamton, New York. What comes to mind are freezing winters and chapped lips. Of course my eventual destiny would be Florida. It was a piece to my puzzle!

My mother's best friend lived next door to us. Her name was Frankie Bangelsdorf. (Is that a great name or what?) I was only a little kid, so you can imagine my delight when Frankie allowed me to go upstairs to her bedroom and play with her five-tiered mahogany jewelry box. Thinking back, perhaps she and my mother just wanted some privacy. Regardless of the reason, it was an enchanting time for me.

My favorite piece of jewelry was a rhinestone-encrusted ballerina pin. When I was wearing that pin, I became a prima ballerina. In my mind's-eye, I was on toe leaping and spinning across the stage as my adoring audience cheered. Ah, the glorious gift of imagination! Sadly, I could not dance then, and I still can't dance!

Frankie died tragically of breast cancer. When she died, I was confused and devastated. I was only a child, seven years old, and yet, I remember feeling this overwhelming need to pray. I can see myself lying on my twin bed, flipping through pages of a Bible.

I remember clearly when I found the 23rd *Psalm*. You know the one: *The LORD is my Shepherd . . .* Why did it resonate with me? I had no way to know that this psalm was read at funerals: I had never been to a funeral. I read and reread that Psalm until I had every word memorized. To this day, I can still recite every word.

What had happened that day? Why did I pick that particular Psalm? In my heart, I believe that was the day my spirituality was born.

When I was eight years old, we moved to Rochester, New York. My parents were born there, and all of our extended family lived in the city. There were thirteen first cousins, all on my mother's side of the family—a clan, best friends who never needed other friends. My surviving cousins, spread from Maryland to Pennsylvania to Florida, have all remained close to this day.

At nine years old, my father announced that I would go to Hebrew school twice a week after regular school. *Gevalt!* I never liked school as a child. I hated sitting still, and I didn't like listening to lectures. I was not a happy camper.

In Hebrew school, the goal was to learn to read and write Hebrew. The weird letters and stranger sounding words made my brain hurt. I remember one phrase very clearly as the teacher spent much of her time saying it, most often to me: *Sheket b'vakasha,* quiet, please! In other words, shut up!

Modern Israel and I were born around the same time. When I think of those years, I still envision pictures of young people dancing in the streets of Israel, their skirts and hair flying. In Hebrew school, they wanted to replicate what our people were doing in the *Eretz Israel.*

And so, every couple of weeks, we would move into the hallways of the school and form large circles of fifteen or more children. The goal was to learn Israeli dancing. The Israeli music lit a fire in my belly that has remained to this day. As for the dancing, like I told you, I was then and still am a *klutz!*

One day the rabbi came and talked to our class. He told us that every one of us would have times in our lives when we were happy and healthy and times when we were sad and sick. He said to try to remember that both were a gift given to us from

G-d. Without the bad times, we would not be able to appreciate the good times. Those words have stayed with me my entire life.

One afternoon, I decided to skip Hebrew school. I joined a bunch of kids from the neighborhood who were sleigh riding down a hill near the synagogue. What a blast I had! The snow was packed solid, and I flew down the hill at what felt like a hundred miles an hour.

As darkness fell, I made my way back to the parking lot of the school to wait for my father to pick me up. When I got in the front seat, he leaned over and kissed me. As the light in the car dimmed to off, I saw a flash of disappointment in his eyes.

"How was Hebrew school?" he asked.

"Great," I replied.

"I guess the heat must have been broken?" he said, obviously baiting me.

I shook my head, knowing I had been caught.

"Perhaps you would like to explain how your cheeks got so red and wind-burned?"

I am sure I got punished, but I can't remember what the punishment was. Whatever it was, it worked. I never skipped Hebrew school again. How I wish I had paid better attention. I would give anything if I could have a do over. Then again, I guess this book is my do over!

CHAPTER 8

MY WORLD DEVOID OF JEWS

When I was eleven, we moved to Naples, Florida with my aunt and uncle and three of my cousins. Per capita, Naples was one of the wealthiest cities in the United States. Families like the Smuckers and the Evinrudes had their winter homes there.

By design, this community of wealthy people chose to live in a society devoid of diversity. The country clubs were even restricted: No Jews, dogs or Blacks.

It was the Sixties and the South still had the Klan, and anti-Semitism was the norm. Our unwelcome arrival brought the Jewish population up to three families. I am sure by now, you must be asking yourself why my parents would have ever moved to such a place? Why else? My Dad and uncle were in the building supply business, and Naples was a wonderful opportunity.

So I traded my winter coat, my extended family and my Judaism for warm weather and sand in my shoes. Most of my new friends had never met or even seen a Jew before we moved to Naples. Many actually believed that Jews had horns.

I was determined to be friendly to everyone in my school: popular, not popular, fat or skinny, rich or poor. The reason: Somewhere down deep inside my self-centered, developing teenage brain, I felt an obligation to change the way my friends perceived Jews. I was convinced if they liked me, they would like all Jews.

I told you, I was a *klutz*. But I was a determined *klutz!* And so, I decided to try out for cheerleading. It was a big deal. They had an assembly, and every girl trying out had to go up on stage and do a cheer. Then the student body voted.

I tripped while doing my routine. I was beyond mortified, but I managed to get through the rest of the cheer. The next day, when the announcements were read, I was named a member of the team. I cried.

Here is what I remember best about being a cheerleader. I got to wear my cheerleading uniform to school for pep rallies. And I got to wear a little silver megaphone on a chain around my neck.

In those years, there were elections for the yearbook: the most likely to succeed, the best dressed, the most popular. To my astonishment, I was elected the most popular. Don't be too impressed—there were only three hundred kids in the entire school.

Regardless of all the nice things that happened to me, this was a complicated time in my life. You see, no matter how hard I tried, these were not my people. Their houses felt different to me, too formal and superficial. Their parents seemed more reserved, less effusive. Worst of all, no one said: *kvetch, oy vey, schlep, gevalt* or even *tushy*.

I remember a friend in sixth grade asking me if I were a Jew or an American. I have no doubt that he heard that discussion at his home, probably more than once. Still, as strange as this may seem, he did not ask me in an anti-Semitic way. Today, I would give the same answer I gave that day: I am both an American and a Jew.

It hurts me to admit this, but in high school, I assimilated into the gentile community. I did not go to church or adapt to their religion;

instead, I buried my Judaism. My soul grieved that loss. It took my father's death, fifty years later, for me to finally embrace fully that which my soul longed for.

CHAPTER 9

BOOKS! BOOKS! BOOKS!

When I began to write this book, I was embarrassed that my Catholic friends in my writing group knew more about biblical Judaism than I knew. They could even quote scripture. I cannot do that, and I would be hard-pressed to find even one of my Jewish friends that could.

But that is okay because I am not pretending to be a scholar. I am a pragmatist, and my goal is to put in plain language the basics of Judaism. I am determined to help the uninitiated, the doubting Jew and the potential convert to understand Judaism in simple terms. My hope is that we will learn together as I try to unravel what is inside my soul. If we can obtain a cursory understanding of the *Torah, Talmud* and the Hebrew Bible and embrace our Judaism, then I will have accomplished what I set out to do.

I believe we learn life's lessons through stories, and I am a storyteller—what I believe to be a precious gift from G-d. This book is my way of saying thank you. I will avoid writing as if you are reading a textbook. If you already have a clear understanding of any subject I cover, you receive a "Get Out of Jail Free" card. Just skip that section and move on!

Judaism is a religion, but it is also the written history of the ancient world. It is a tribute to a people that, despite all odds, continue to strive and survive regardless of past or present travails. I believe, to understand Judaism we must also understand its history. And that begins with the *Torah*.

Torah—also called the **Chumash.** I know, I know, I know. Why does it have to have two names? Thing is, you will hear it referred to by both names, and I don't want you to get confused. For our purposes, I will stick to the word *Torah*.

The *Torah* is the Five Books of Moses. Five separate books, all written on the parchment scroll that make up the *Torah: Genesis, Exodus, Leviticus, Numbers* and *Deuteronomy.*

Think of *Torah* as the main event. It is the foundation of Judaism that all else stands upon. Above all else, *Torah* is a *document of faith*. I say this because if we start to apply carbon dating, archeology, chronology etc. to the *Torah*, we will find ourselves lost, confused and doubting. I hope that you will join me by embracing your intellectual mind and your spirituality.

Moses declared that no more than three days should ever pass without giving honor to the *Torah*. Consequently, we read *Torah* in the synagogue on Monday, Thursday and Saturday. To do so, there must be a *minyan*. A *minyan* requires ten men in Orthodoxy. In Conservative and Reform, women are counted in the *minyan*. *Torah* is also read on holidays; fast days and on the new moon.

The first time I was in services and they announced prayer for the new moon (*Rosh Chodesh*), I remember thinking: not *another* reason for the services to be longer? I am a bit embarrassed to admit that only in the past year, have I come to love these special prayers. Perhaps that is because the passing of each month reminds me to cherish every day in my fleeting life: It is Monday, and then it is Friday and then it is

Monday again! I am not complaining. I have lived long enough to know that when illness strikes, a day can feel like an eternity.

Rosh Chodesh reminds me that another month has passed in my life. It reminds me to live in the moment and to value each day. Perhaps this is one of the reasons that we celebrate holidays: They mark the passage of time and remind us of our mortality.

Walking into a synagogue can be daunting. Many of you will know the rituals that make up a service. For those of you who do not know or may have forgotten, here is an overview.

Before the *Torah* reading, the *Torah* is removed from the *Aron haKodesh,* the Holy Ark. We stand as the *Torah* is carried around the room. People kiss it with either their prayer book or with the fringe on their *tallit,* the prayer shawl. Regardless of how many times I participate in this ritual, it always feels holy, hurling me back in time, connecting me for a millisecond with my history and my people.

The *Torah* is then placed on the *bimah,* a podium that usually stands on a raised platform in the front of the synagogue. Each week a portion from the *Torah,* known as a *parshah,* is read.

There are fifty-four portions that we read, and this includes leap years. I will explain the leap years and the Hebrew calendar later in the book. Over the course of a year, we read from the book of *Genesis* through to the book of *Deuteronomy.* In other words, we read portions from every book of the *Torah.*

Various members of the congregation are given the honor to come forward and participate in the readings. This honor is known as an *Aliyah.* The first *Aliyah* is given to a *Kohein* or Cohen if one is present. *Kohein* in Hebrew translates to priest. The name Cohen designates someone who is a patrilineal (descended from the line of the father), descendant of Moses' brother, Aaron. Aaron's descendants were the priests who oversaw the altar and the sacrifices when the Jews were in the desert and during the First and Second Temple periods.

The second *Aliyah* is given to a Levi, if one is present. Levi was one of the Twelve Tribes of Israel. When Moses was on Mt. Sinai, and the Jews lost faith and constructed the idol of the golden calf, the tribe of Levi did not participate. That is why, to this day, they are still honored with the second *Aliyah*.

The rest of *Aliyah*s are given out as honors to a person who may be celebrating special events in their lives, a visitor, or someone who goes to the synagogue often.

For the *Aliyah*, congregants come to the *bimah*. They use their *tallit* to touch the first word of the section to be read in the *Torah* scroll. Many will then kiss their *tallit*. The congregant then chants a blessing for the reading of the Torah. The transliteration is always available for those who cannot read Hebrew.

The rabbi, cantor or a learned member of the congregation then reads from the *Torah* scrolls. No vowels appear in the *Torah*, so even if you can read Hebrew, the reading is unbelievably difficult. Just think how hard and long a Bar or Bat Mitzvah student studies to read one small portion.

After the *Torah* portion is read on Shabbat, we also read a passage from the *Prophets* known as the *Haftarah*. The reading from the *Haftarah* always relates in some way to that week's *Torah* portion.

The ark that holds the *Torah* scroll, the holiest place in the synagogue, is situated in the front of the synagogue on the Eastern wall. This is so the congregation will face the holy city of Jerusalem when they pray.

Before the *Torah* scroll is returned to the ark, a congregant or rabbi will lift the open *Torah* scroll high above his or her head. You may have seen a picture of this, if you have not seen it in synagogue. The scroll is heavy and often not equally distributed.

It is a moment that always makes me catch my breath. For me, it is a symbol of the resilience of the Jewish nation: Regardless of all those attempts to destroy us, we are still a proud people. We are still here!

CHAPTER 10

LET'S MEET THE BOOKS OF *TORAH*

Genesis

The first book is *Genesis*: The beginning of creation: Adam and Eve, Noah and the flood, the generations of Abraham, the binding of Jacob, Isaac's son. Jacob is the third patriarch and his twin brother is Esau. Jacob steals Esau's birthright. We read about the birth of Jacob's twelve sons and one daughter and the story of Joseph, one of Jacob's sons, the eleventh. We are introduced to murder, the first flood and the first organized rebellion.

To quote Rabbi Boruch Clinton: "This is the book about the way the world was built, its rules and purpose, its people, both great and small."

Exodus

The second book is *Exodus*: The story of Moses and his family, the ten plagues, the exodus from Egypt and the parting of the Reed Sea (not the Red Sea). The *Torah* says G-d took the people in a roundabout path. . . .to the *Yam Suf*, Sea of Reeds. (*Exodus:* 13:18). If you want to look really smart, call it the Reed Sea, just know, almost everyone else calls it the Red Sea.

Exodus includes Moses receiving the Ten Commandments at Mt. Sinai and the Jews wandering in the wilderness for forty years and building the Tabernacle that held the Ten Commandments. The Tabernacle was the place where G-d communicated with Moses when the Jews were wandering the desert. It was a portable sanctuary that could be constructed, taken down and rebuilt as the Jews wandered in the desert.

Passover was born in the book of *Exodus*: the holiday that celebrates Israel's liberation from Egyptian slavery. Regardless of where I am on my Jewish journey, Passover has always been a constant. It seems to be the one holiday that even the most assimilated Jews will often celebrate. Perhaps it is because the entire Jewish nation saw the miracle as we stood together on the shore when the waters of the Reed Sea parted.

My earliest memories of Passover are as clear to me today as if they had happened but a moment ago. I can see my grandmother, my aunts and my mother washing the kosher for Passover dishes and then setting the tables. I can wander back to the scents of bubbling chicken soup, brisket and turkey roasting and *tzimis* warming on the stove. I can still taste the love.

At the Passover service, my Grandpa Leonard was very strict. He would not tolerate any side conversations during the reading of the *Haggadah*, the Passover prayer book.

Mistake number one: All thirteen cousins were relegated to the kids' table. Did they really expect us to behave? Someone was always breaking Grandpa's rules by whispering or sneaking a piece of matzo before the proper time in the service. Invariably, fingers were stuck into the horseradish as we tried not to gag!

My favorite part of the service was dipping my knife into the cup of red wine and then tapping the wine onto the plate ten times to represent blood and the ten plagues: blood, frogs, locusts, etc. Ugh!

The youngest child at the *Seder* always got to read the Four Questions in Hebrew. The Four Questions expound on why Passover is different from all other nights. The youngest always needed help, and that is where I came in. I loved showing off how perfectly I knew the Hebrew! I think it was the only thing I learned in Hebrew school.

My grandfather, of blessed memory, insisted that we read every word in the *Hagaddah*. We moaned and *kvetched* and couldn't wait to eat. Today many of us abbreviate the service. My grandfather would not approve. Is it wrong? I don't know, but what I do know is: A majority of Jews still celebrate, honor and remember this event even though it took place thousands of years ago. Good for us!

Passover is a time for us to reflect and remember and celebrate our freedom. It was not that long ago that the Nazis attempted to annihilate the Jews. Because we survived we have the right to make choices in our lives, to contemplate what path we will follow and what words we will speak. Let those words be ones of hope, peace and justice for all the people that inhabit our planet.

CHAPTER 11

SO MANY JEWS IN THE DESERT!

Leviticus

The third book is *Leviticus*: This book serves as a roadmap. In Leviticus we read: Love your fellow as yourself. We are instructed how to live as a holy nation and how to properly worship G-d.

There is a lot to read about that! *Leviticus* includes rules for the priesthood, ritual purity, animal sacrifices, dietary laws, (more about that in *Deuteronomy*), *Yom Kippur* and all the festivals, ownership of land and indebtedness. There are six hundred thirteen commandments interspersed in the Five Books of Moses—two hundred and forty-six of those commandments are found in *Leviticus*.

Numbers

The fourth book is *Numbers*: *Numbers* is the narrative that starts where *Exodus* leaves off. The book is the story of the years the Jews wandered in the desert. It tells of the beginning years and the later years, but there is little commentary on the thirty-eight years in between.

Numbers begins with a census. There were six hundred thousand Jewish males between the ages of twenty and sixty in the Sinai. This was not a guess. Each name was listed and every clan accounted for. Add women and children and elders to that number, and we begin to get the picture of just how many millions of our people were in that desert!

Numbers is also about rebellion: the shortage of meat, fear of entering Israel, the leadership of Moses, complaints about lack of water and how our men were drawn into the enticements of the daughters of Moav. The Book of *Numbers* tells the end of the journey that began in Egypt.

We are now coming to the fifth and final book of the *Torah*. Whew! I know it was intense, but I promise you, I did my best to give you a quick overview. It was not easy to do. I had to leave out some really cool stuff.

Deuteronomy

This book covers the final weeks of Moses' life just before our entry into the land of Israel. Moses gave a long and fiery farewell speech to his people shortly before his death. He beseeched the Jews to follow the commandments in the *Torah*. "*Watch yourselves **very** carefully, lest you should slip; lest you should fail to keep even the most obvious of commandments.*" *(Deuteronomy8:11)*

There are one hundred and ninety-nine new commandments in *Deuteronomy*, but many are ideas mentioned in other books of the *Torah*. This book stresses monotheism, the belief in one G-d and the loyalty that Israel owes G-d. *Deuteronomy* foreshadows our life in the land of Israel, stipulating that sacrifices to the LORD may only take place in the religious capital, in a single sanctuary.

As Jews, we do not have a shortage of blessings. We pray upon waking, sleeping, before and after eating, when we go on a trip and when we return. In fact, every rite of passage, from birth to death, is replete with prayers.

And yet, there are only two prayers written in the *Torah* that are required to be said when not in the Holy Temple. They both appear in

Deuteronomy: grace after meals and the *Shema*. One prayer is reminding us to be thankful that we have nourishment.

The other prayer, the *Shema*, is the touchstone of Judaism. As is our duty, we sing out our vow to the LORD that we will have only One G-d.

Hear, Israel, *the LORD is our God, the LORD is One. Sh'ma Yisra'eil Adonai Eloheinu Adonai echad.*

The *Shema* calls for us to open our ears and thereby our hearts and listen so that the words of this prayer will always be remembered.

The prayer is so holy to us as a people that the *Shema* is supposed to be the last words on our lips before dying.

CHAPTER 12

WHAT REALLY HAPPENED IN THAT DESERT?

It is less than four hundred miles from the border of Egypt to the land of Israel and yet, the Jews wandered the Sinai Desert for forty years. Have you ever wondered why it took so long? Where did they go? What did they do? Let us begin at Mount Sinai.

I learned about Moses and the Ten Commandments from Charlton Heston. I can still see him holding the stone tablets over his head with the wind whipping and the thunder crashing. Years later, I learned about the Ark of the Covenant from Indiana Jones (Harrison Ford) in the movie *Raiders of the Lost Ark*. Perhaps, these were not the best places to learn about Judaism.

Let your imagination soar. Three million Jews have been freed from Egypt and are traversing the Sinai desert. Three months into their journey, they camp near Mt. Sinai. Moses climbs the mountain, and G-d speaks to him:

So shall you say to the house of Jacob and tell the sons of Israel. You have seen what I did to the Egyptians, and [how] I bore you on eagles' wings, and I brought you to Me. And now, if you obey Me and keep My covenant, you shall be to Me a treasure out of all peoples, for Mine is the entire earth. And you shall be to Me a kingdom of princes and a holy nation (*Exodus* 19:3).

Moses came back down the mountain with G-d's words in his heart. He called the elders together and repeated G-d's message. The elders vowed to obey and to keep the covenant without knowing what that promise entailed.

Hearing their unconditional acceptance, G-d told Moses to prepare the people for His presence. He warned that any man or beast would die if they approached Mt. Sinai because that was where G-d would appear. Dark ominous clouds descended over the mountain. Thunder shook the ground, and lightning streaked across the sky. Above all the noise, a *shofar*, (ram's horn) was heard. Then there was complete and absolute silence.

From the silence, a voice emerged—G-d's voice. Every man, woman and child heard G-d's words demanding that the Jewish people follow His Ten Commandments.

Can we put ourselves in that moment? Can we even begin to contemplate what it would be like to hear G-d's voice at the same time that millions of others were also hearing His voice?

The people were terrified of the incomparable power of the LORD. They begged Moses to become their intermediary. It is said that Moses knew that G-d had revealed Himself to the people so that they would *fear* Him and not sin. We commemorate the day we are given the Ten Commandments with the holiday of *Shavuot*. *Shavuot* takes place seven weeks after Passover.

Moses ascended Mt. Sinai for a second time. He remained for forty days and forty nights. Forty days and nights is a very long time when you are waiting around for someone to come back. If we allow ourselves to contemplate why the Jews lost faith, I think we can begin to understand. Or can we?

G-d had freed the Jews from slavery, and then He actually allowed them to be in His presence: to hear His voice and His commandments. Did that keep the Jews loyal and G-d fearing? Do human beings ever learn?

In their doubt and probably fear, the masses turned to Aaron, Moses' older brother. Needing to feel some solace in a G-d they could see and touch, they insisted that Aaron make them an idol! Aaron acquiesced and instructed the people to bring him all of their gold. Aaron had the gold melted and then fashioned a golden calf (or small bull) to worship.

When Moses came down off the mountain and saw the people worshiping an idol, he was inconsolable. He berated Aaron. In his fury, Moses threw the tablets of the Ten Commandments to the ground. They shattered. As a punishment, Moses had the golden calf melted. When the liquid gold dried, he had it ground into a powder. He then had the people drink the powdered god so that there was nothing left of their idol. Some died from ingesting the drink.

G-d told Moses that the Jews would have to die for their great sin. After all, He had just appeared before the people, and the Second Commandment was very clear. *You shall not have other G-d's before Me* (*Exodus* 20:3). Moses beseeched G-d to forgive the Jews and give them another chance. He pleaded: *You brought them out from Egypt. They are yours.*

G-d relented but insisted that the most brazen idolaters were to pay with their lives. Three thousand Israelites were slain. Their deaths were carried out by the Levites, the only tribe that did not participate in the idolatry. To this day, as we learned a few pages ago, the Levites(surname Levi) are still honored for their loyalty by being called to the *Torah* for the second *Alyiah*.

CHAPTER 13

TAKING ISSUE!

I have to stop here and take issue. First of all, G-d told Moses that the Jews would be forgiven. If that was so, why did a horrible plague soon follow, where thousands of Jews perished? So much for being forgiven.

There is another question that absolutely baffles me. Why wasn't Aaron punished? After all, he led the people in building the idol. Not only was Aaron not punished; he was rewarded.

Aaron eventually was appointed the High Priest of the Jewish people: the only man alive who could approach the Holy of Holies and live, as he did only on *Yom Kippur*.

The rabbis offer us an explanation. They purport that Aaron oversaw the building of the golden calf to appease the people. His intention was to keep the Jewish nation from rioting until Moses returned from the mountain. The rabbis maintain that Aaron believed his brother Moses' return would prove to the Jews that G-d was and would always be there for the House of Israel.

The Jews in that desert, while waiting for Moses to return, *needed to feel solace in a G-d they could not touch!*

Before ascending Mt. Sinai for a third time, Moses instructed the Jews to mourn the death of their three thousand brethren, who had been killed by the Levites. Moses commanded them to repent for their sin of idolatry, by fasting from sunrise until sunset every day until his return. This later became the holiday of *Yom Kippur*.

Moses spent another forty days and forty nights without food or sleep. It is said he had become like an angel. During that time, G-d again inscribed the Tablets with the Ten Commandments. God also revealed the entire *Torah* to Moses: the six hundred and thirteen commandments along with the laws and the interpretations. The *Torah* was taught orally to Moses by G-d because the written *Torah* would have been incomprehensible without G-d's teachings.

Moses would spend the rest of his life teaching the *Oral Torah* given directly to him by G-d. The *Torah* is our story, the story of Judaism told and retold, allowing those that hear the teachings to ask questions and learn—just as it was then and just as it is now, thousands of years later.

When I look at the story of Mt. Sinai and think about how the Jews thought Moses had deserted them, I see it as an analogy for the times in my own life, when I thought G-d had forsaken me.

In my twenties, I was desperate, depressed and terrified. I had three children under seven, and I was in a verbally abusive and miserable marriage. When I look back, which I don't do often, I can't believe how unhappy I was.

I took diet pills. They were the rage in the seventies. They gave me an inflated feeling of well being so that I could make it through the day, do the laundry, make the beds, put on my make-up and go to the grocery store. No one knew then that speed was addictive.

One day, I realized I couldn't get out of bed without the pill. The day that I put that pill down was the day I decided to change my life. The marriage had to end! I had no money, and I had never worked. But, I had my parents, and they stepped in to save me. And I mean that literarily.

G-d was nowhere in my conscious life then. Yet, I felt empowered. I remember having this overwhelming feeling that I could be anything I wanted to be, if I had the courage to try. I told my sister-in-law," I don't know how, but I am telling you, I am going to be a success!" The moment those words were spoken something shifted in my life. I could feel G-d's presence even if it would be years before I would begin a journey to embrace my religion.

CHAPTER 14

THE MIRACLE OF REPLICATION!

I remember a game we played as children, *Telephone*. We would sit in a circle, and someone would whisper something. The person would repeat what they had heard to the next person in the circle. On and on, it would go. By the time the last person heard the message it had changed.

And yet, the spoken *Torah* stayed accurate as it was disseminated to millions of Jews. How did the information remain so exact? Every *Torah* scroll ever produced is the exact replica of the previous *Torah*. This alone is a miracle.

Regardless of where Jews are in our history, one fundamental belief has remained unchanged and is the basis of Judaism: **The *Torah* and the Ten Commandments came directly from G-d.**

That being the truth, wouldn't that mean that G-d had also revealed to Moses when he would die? After all, the last book of the *Torah*, *Deuteronomy*, foretells Moses' death and highlights our entering the land of Israel.

You will read and hear various opinions from our most learned rabbis and biblical scholars on this question. There are those that say the *Torah* was not even written while the Jews were in the desert. I prefer to believe that the last book in the *Torah, Deuteronomy,* was not revealed to Moses until he was nearing the end of his journey in the desert. At that time, Moses wrote the closing verses of the *Torah*, and his brother, Aaron wrote the final descriptions that included the death of Moses.

I visualize Moses as he sat in his tent surrounded by the great Jewish minds of his time. He is teaching them the intricacies of the *Torah*, as given to him by G-d. On this particular day, I visualize Moses speaking about the rules of the Sabbath, admonishing that it is G-d's commandment that we keep and remember *Shabbat*. He quotes from the *Torah* that we must rest on the seventh day from work, and even our servants and domesticated animals must have a day of total rest. He instructs them that no fire can be kindled on the Sabbath.

I can hear the questions that must have followed: *Tell us Moses, what constitutes rest? What are the rules about cooking when we cannot light a fire? Must we dress a certain way? Are we allowed to write? Are there topics we cannot discuss?*

I see them talking until darkness descends as Moses answers each question just as G-d had taught him. I believe Moses spoke with great patience, smiling, intuiting that for thousands of years, the ever-resilient Jews would adapt whatever rules necessary to maintain the laws of the Sabbath.

Four years into my Jewish journey, a lot has changed as it pertains to the Sabbath. My husband and I now try to stay home on Friday night. I set a fancy table in the dining room and use my good silver and china. Even though I feel good about doing this, I don't feel that good! Why? My home is not kosher, although I do not eat or serve any of the forbidden food. Jewish guilt is not a made up concept. It is real. I am walking, talking proof of that.

I have begun a tradition in my family that I want to share with you. Every Friday night, I take a picture of my Shabbat table. I light the Shabbat candles, and then I light six tea candles to represent each of our children's families. Sometimes that photo includes my husband. Sometimes it will include a grandchild that may be visiting. I then text the photo, to each of our children and grandchildren: Yes, I am that savvy.

Here is the most exciting thing that happens next. I get texts back from the youngest to the oldest. Sometimes it is just a smiley face or an "I love you." And sometimes, it is a picture of one of them lighting candles with their family! How great is that? It makes my heart sing! This is my way of reminding my family that we are Jews!

My husband Mel and I go to synagogue on most Saturdays, and then we hang out at home. I have instituted a few rules for myself. If we go out, I do not shop or spend money. I do not read e-mails or turn on my computer until 5 o'clock in the evening.

Strangely, something mysterious has begun to happen to me. I have always been one to run until I drop. It is not unusual for me to have three separate plans during one day, and often I do. And yet, I now look forward to the Sabbath. I feel myself taking a deep breath and telling myself that I don't have to do anything. Just stop. Calm down. Breathe.

Am I doing everything I am supposed to do on the Sabbath? Not even close. I could make the list of things I do wrong, and they would fill a page. But I have taken a tiny step forward. Perhaps one day, I will do more. Or maybe this is as far as I will go. For now, it is enough for me. It is a giant step I never imagined I would take.

CHAPTER 15

SETTING THE STAGE FOR THE *MISHNAH*

King Solomon built the First Temple around 827 BCE. The Temple was at the center of Jewish life and stood for **four hundred and ten years**. During the time the Temple stood, the Assyrians managed to conquer the Southern Kingdom of Judea, (from Jerusalem south to Beersheba) and the Northern Kingdom (from Jericho north to Galilee and the Golan Heights.) They forced the most intelligent and wealthy Jews to resettle elsewhere, believing that scattering the Jews would finally put an end to them.

How wrong they were! We may have been fickle when we built the golden calf, but as a people, we were resilient and determined to survive! Even after the Babylonians destroyed the First Temple, and even after Alexander the Great conquered Judea, the Jews maintained their commitment to One G-d.

Construction on the Second Temple began seventy years after the destruction of the First Temple. The Second Temple stood for **four hundred and twenty years**. Think about this for a moment. The First and Second Temples stood in the holy city of Jerusalem, where the Dome of the Rock now stands, for over eight hundred years!

In 37 CE, Rome conquered Israel, and Herod the Great came to power. Known as the great builder, Herod enlarged and refurbished the Second Temple. He also built the maritime port of Caesarea and the Fortress of Masada. But he was a tyrannical ruler, mistreating his workers and murdering anyone who stood against him.

After Herod's death, the economy of Israel lay in ruins. What resulted were riots against the burden of heavy taxes. The High Priests of the Holy Temple, Jonathan and Ananias were murdered. The First Jewish War ensued. That war ended with the Romans killing thousands of Jews and destroying the Second Temple.

Some forty years later, the Jews rebelled against Rome in a campaign known as the Bar Kochba Revolt. We learned earlier about Bar Kochba, a false Messiah, who led the Jews in defeating the Roman army.

Rome was humiliated that a rag tag army of Jewish zealots had defeated them. In response, they eventually attacked with the full force of their army. Over a million Jews were massacred. The Jews that survived were sent into exile.

Rabbi Yehuda Hansasi, known as Judah the Prince, was terrified that after the Bar Kochba Revolt we might lose the Oral *Torah*. He feared that the horrific massacre and consequent scattering of our people would cause us to forget.

Judah the Prince decided to put quill and ink to the words of G-d. This great man, wealthy beyond description and a friend to emperors, framed and edited a book that became known as the *Mishnah*. The Hebrew definition of *mishnah* is study by repetition.

It was a massive undertaking, gathering the writings from hundreds of rabbis across the generations and then editing, explaining and organizing those writings into the *Mishnah*. The *Mishnah* is a greatly shortened version of the Oral *Torah*, certainly the *CliffsNotes* version when compared to the books that would follow it.

The writings in the *Mishnah* were contributed by an academy of great scholars. They lived from 100 BCE-200 CE, all experts in specific areas of the Oral *Torah*. Some were experts on the Sabbath, others on tort (civil) law and damages, etc. They were not much different from our doctors and lawyers who specialize today. *Mishnah* is written in classic Hebrew, often times magnificently concise and other times, cryptic and hidden.

The book covers six main subjects:

1) Prayers, blessings and agriculture laws.
2) Sabbath and the holiday laws.
3) Women, issues of marriage and divorce.
4) Civil and criminal law.
5) The Temple, dietary laws and sacrifices.
6) Laws of purity and impurity.

I think it is fair to say that Judah the Prince's genius was in his ability to organize the *Mishna* systematically by subject. Before the *Mishnah*, if you wanted to know about the Sabbath, you would have had to memorize every place it was mentioned in the *Torah*. In the *Mishnah*, the Rabbi had a heading for the Sabbath where you could find all the doctrine in one place.

Tucked inside the pages of the *Mishnah* is the book known as *Pirkei Avot, The Ethics of the Fathers*. I would do a great injustice if I did not include a few of the proverbs and sayings found in the first chapter of this book.

The world stands on three things: Torah, the service of G-d, and deeds of kindness.

Let your home be a meeting place for the wise; dust yourself in the soil of their feet, and drink thirstily of their words.

Distance yourself from a bad neighbor, do not cleave to a wicked person, and do not abandon belief in retribution.

Love work, loath mastery over others, and avoid intimacy with the government. (Perhaps our politicians could use a bit of this teaching?)

And the most famous of all: *If I am not for myself, who is for me? And if I am only for myself, what am I? And if not now, when?*

Much of the *Mishnah* is dry legal recitation. Judah the Prince knew that, but he was determined to inspire later generations. He told stories and added minority views that he knew would lead to enlivened commentary.

Enlivened commentary. When did Jews ever need an excuse for that?

CHAPTER 16

THE EXPLAINERS PUT IT IN WRITING

In the centuries following the *Mishnah,* the rabbis began to worry that the deeper meanings of the Oral *Torah* were being lost. These rabbis were known as explainers. They had been recording their opinions and discussions on the Oral *Torah* and the *Mishnah* and then passing them down. Remember, the *Torah* was so difficult to understand that even Moses had to be taught directly from G-d.

The books that emerged from those writings are known as the *Talmud.* There are six thousand two hundred pages in the books of the *Talmud.* If we were to study just one page a day, and that would be a feat, it would take seven years to read the entire *Talmud.* Thousands of Jews do study a page of the Talmud daily and at the end of the seven-year cycle there is a worldwide celebration.

There were actually two *Talmuds* written: one by a group of rabbis in Babylonia (Iraq), and the other by rabbis in Jerusalem (actually Tiberius). Unfortunately, due to Roman and then Christian persecution, the *Jerusalem Talmud* was never finished. We study the *Babylonian Talmud,* but the *Jerusalem Talmud* is still studied by some.

Here is what you need to know: **When Jews study Judaism, we do not study *Torah*—we study *Talmud.***

I know what comes next is a bit confusing. It was to me as well. Just hang in with me for several more lines, while I explain how the *Talmud* is laid out. First let me show you a picture:

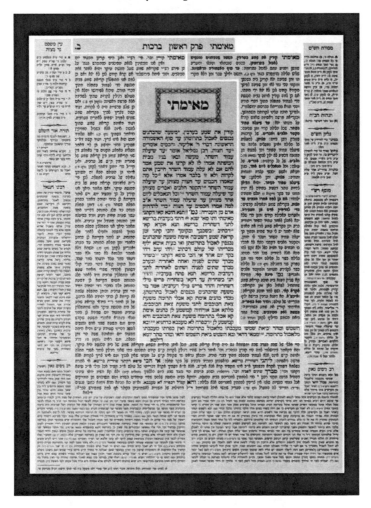

What you see in the center of this page are writings from the *Mishnah* written by Judah the Prince and writings from the *Gemara*. All the writings surrounding it are opinions and commentaries from the rabbis over the generations.

The writings of the *Mishnah* and the *Gemara* make up the *Talmud*, all six thousand two hundred pages. *Gemara* in Hebrew means completion, and in Aramaic it means tradition. *Mishnah* in Hebrew means study by repetition.

Recap: Basically, the *Talmud* includes arguments and stories offered by rabbis in different time periods of Judaism. Commentaries were added as late as 1,000 CE -1,500 CE by names of rabbis you may actually be familiar with: Rashi, Maimonides and Nachmanides.

Talmud is made up of the *Mishnah* and the *Gemara*. See, not so hard to grasp. And by the way, you will probably hear some refer to the *Talmud* as the *Mishnah* and others the *Gemara*. Don't let that throw you. They are all speaking basically about the same thing: *Talmud.*

As you can see from the picture of the *Talmud* page, learning is non-linear and multi-layered. No wonder the scholars spend a lifetime with these books. Over the last one thousand years, it is not the *Torah* but the *Talmud* that the enemies of the Jewish people have consistently searched for and burned.

With all the enemies that we have had throughout history, wouldn't you think as a people, we would be united in what we believe about the basics of our religion? I thought so too but . . .

I was sitting in Shabbat services one day listening to a Reform rabbi say that perhaps the Exodus was nothing more than a myth like *The Wizard of Oz*. At this point, I was still a member of a Reform congregation.

At first, I thought I must have misunderstood. I had just finished writing about Moses in the desert and how millions of our people had witnessed the miracles. Now, a Reform rabbi was telling me that it was a fable, a *bubba meisah*! How dare he? I felt as though I had been personally assaulted—a baby Jew just learning to walk slammed off her feet! Where were these emotions coming from?

The next morning at the Conservative services I still attended daily, I told the rabbi what had transpired and how upset I was. I expected him to be incensed as well. Instead, he was calm and gentle. He pointed out that perhaps there was a need for a rabbi like that, a rabbi who would draw people into Judaism, people who believed as he did. I was flabbergasted. I did not want the rabbi to be so rational. It made me crazy! We either have faith all the way, or we don't really have faith? Right?

As I was leaving the synagogue, the rabbi said softly, "As for me, I believe that every letter and word in the *Torah* was inspired by G-d." Yeah, Rabbi Marc!

As fate would have it, that night we went out to dinner with new friends from South Africa. They keep a kosher home, and the husband puts on *Tefillin* in his home every day. *Tefillin* are cube-shaped black leather boxes that contain four scriptural passages. These boxes are attached to the head and arm by black leather straps and worn by men (and some women) during the morning prayers.

I told my new friends what the Reform rabbi had said, again expecting a great discussion on how terrible his remarks were. Instead I heard: "I don't believe the *Torah* was written in the desert either." *Oy gevalt!* This is a man I really respected as a Jew. Yet, as I listened, instead of being angry, I felt as if a window had opened, and the breezes of acceptance were stirring my self-righteous indignation.

Here was my takeaway.

I am on a raft drifting across uncharted seas. Some days are calm, and I am lulled. Other days, I am forced to hold on for dear life. Across that journey, I need to remember: My beliefs belong to me. My rational mind tells me that there is much to question as to when and who wrote the *Torah*. But my heart and soul see it differently: I believe that every word was inspired by G-d. How else could those exact words have survived for thousands of years?

Chapter 17

IS DEATH THE END?

I am going to hit the pause button and shift gears. We will go back to the Hebrew Bible later.

I think for that first year, as I sat during daily services to say *Kaddish* for my father, all I did was try and recognize the Hebrew words and stay on the right page. I would read the English once in a while, but most of the time, I was in a fugue state, shut down and shut off. Whatever feelings I had, had been shoved down so deep I couldn't have accessed them if I wanted to. I knew I was in synagogue to heal from my grief, and I guess that happens differently for different people.

At home, I tried to act normal. And the normal me always had plenty to say about other people. Whenever I would say something judgmental or nasty about someone in my life, my husband would ask, "Want to tell me what you are getting out of synagogue?"

How could I tell him the truth? I was simply taking up a seat.

Then one morning, I got to synagogue early and sat with the prayer book in my hand. I read a prayer that was on the page before the beginning of the service. I read the line, *G-d of my forefathers, Master of all works, LORD of all souls, Blessed are You, Ha'Shem, Who restores souls* to *dead bodies*. (*Ha'Shem* translates as "the name." It is another word for G-d).

I felt as though I had awakened from a stupor. What did this mean? Were there other places in the *Siddur* where awakening the dead could be found? I turned pages frantically scanning the words. I found another prayer, one I had skimmed over a hundred times without taking the meaning into my heart: *Who sustains the living with kindness,* ***resuscitates the dead with abundant mercy,*** *supports the fallen, heals the sick, releases the confined, and maintains His faith to those asleep in the dust. Who is like You, O Master of mighty deeds, and who is comparable to You, O King* ***Who caused death and restores life and makes salvation sprout!***

And You are faithful to resuscitate the dead. Blessed are You, Ha'Shem, Who resuscitates the dead.

Resuscitates the dead: brings them back to life! Did that mean if I prayed hard enough, I could bring my father back, my mother? I knew that was ridiculous, but what did it mean?

When my granddaughter, Emma, was born two months after my mother passed away, we all felt sure she had my mother's soul. When my daughter gave birth to her son, Jacob, three months after my father passed away, we all felt that connection again, this time with my father's soul.

The amazing thing about these two children, separated in age by seven years, is that when they are in the same room they are inseparable— just as my parents had been. Jacob only wants to play with Emma, and he has been like that since he was a baby.

I have always believed that death is like birth. Imagine a baby floating and growing inside its mother's belly. It is safe, warm and well fed. But soon the baby begins to outgrow its home and knows that there is only one way out. Imagine how terrified that baby feels now. It looks down the birth canal and thinks; *there is no way I am getting out of here alive.*

Conversely, every day that we live takes a toll on our bodies. We all know that someday our bodies will no longer be able to sustain us. We know that death is inevitable, but we find this truth hard to grasp. We don't know what will be coming next. I have always chosen to believe that death is simply a rebirth. I never knew until that morning that my belief was a belief also held in Judaism.

CHAPTER 18

REINCARNATION. REALLY?

I told Rabbi Marc that I was writing a chapter in my book about rein-carnation and angels.

"Let me show you something," he said, taking out two *Artscroll Siddurs*, the Orthodox prayer book.

I am a bit ashamed to admit that my first thought was, *"Ok Ellen, you have officially gone over the edge. Next thing you'll be doing is quoting scripture!"*

Here I was sitting with the rabbi, studying scripture. I almost heard my father applauding. And the most amazing part, once I moved into the moment and let go of my preconceived ideas, I found myself really enjoying the discussion. It was pretty cool. (I know that expression dates me. But it is from my generation, and it is the perfect expression for what I was feeling.)

The rabbi had me turn to the Bedtime *Shema* (prayer). I grew up saying: *"Now I lay me down to sleep."* The one the rabbi was showing me, I had never read before. I was going to include just the part of the prayer that pertained to our reincarnation topic, but it is so magnificent, I can't leave out even one word.

*Master of the universe, I hereby forgive anyone who angered or antagonized me or who sinned against me—whether against my body, my property, my honor or against anything of mine: whether he did so accidentally, willfully, carelessly or purposely; whether through speech, deed, thought, or notion; whether in this **transmigration** or another **transmigration**— I forgive every Jew. May no man be punished because of me. May it be Your will, Ha'Shem, my G-d and the G-d of my forefathers, that I may sin no more. Whatever sins I have done before You, may You blot out in Your abundant mercies, but not through suffering or bad illnesses. May the expressions of my mouth and the thoughts of my heart find favor before You, Ha'Shem, my Rock and my Redeemer.*

Transmigration: I certainly had never heard the word before. Transmigration is a translation from the Hebrew word *gilgul*, referring to the doctrine of transmigration of souls, or the recycling of souls, if that makes it easier to understand. The idea comes from one of the most mystical doctrines in Kabalistic literature. It refers to the soul reincarnating for physical life on earth.

The *Talmud* alludes to a mystical school of thought. Just like the Oral *Torah*, these teachings were not written down until the Middle Ages when Rabbi Shimon Bar Yochai wrote the *Zohar*. The *Zohar* is a mystical book that is an integral part of Kabalistic literature. I venture to say that most of us had never even heard of *Kabbalah* before Madonna came on the scene and made it so popular.

Reincarnation is a Kabalistic belief system embraced by Orthodox and Ultra- Orthodox Jews. I have to admit that having never been taught anything about reincarnation makes me a bit angry. I cannot help but feel left out—as though there was a delicious piece of cake waiting for me to take a bite.

I think it is important that we have a clear understanding of Orthodoxy before we move ahead, since they are the ones who have held staunchly to this belief of reincarnation.

Orthodox Jews believe they are the authentic Jews. I am not going into what that makes the rest of us who are not Orthodox. It does not matter to me. I respect this group for carrying on the religion in the manner that they do. It takes an unyielding commitment. So, I say *mazel tov* and wish them all great blessings.

There are two distinct groups in Orthodoxy. One group believes that their lives can be compatible with the society around them. They will live among us while maintaining their religious and cultural values. This group includes Modern Orthodox and Religious Zionists.

The second group is known as the ultra-Orthodox (*Haredim*). They see present day culture as a direct threat to their way of life. They will work beside us, but their communities are separated from our society. Their lives are filled with *Torah* study, prayer and family. There is no television, movies, Internet or secular reading. The ultra-Orthodox men dress in black suits and black velvet *yarmulkes* or black hats. They have beards and *payot* (sidelocks). Women dress very modestly and once married, they cover their heads with wigs, hats or scarves.

Now back to reincarnation. Below are a few scriptural passages that allude to reincarnation. Let's look at the Book of *Job*. (We will get to examine this book later.)

Behold, all these things does G-d do—twice, even three times with a man—to bring his soul back from the pit that he may be enlightened with the light of the living. (Job 33:29)

Does this refer to G-d allowing a person to come back from death and try again?

Another example from the bible is in Daniel 12:13: *now go your way to the end and rest, and you shall arise to your destiny at the end of days.*

According to the *Zohar* 1186b, *As long as a person is unsuccessful in his purpose in this world, the Holy One, blessed be He, uproots him and replants him over and over again.*

You decide what you believe. But let me share with you the philosophy of the Orthodox and see if it resonates with you. The best way to do this is for me to just give you a direct quote from the *Zohar:*

All souls are subject to reincarnation; and people do not know the ways of the Holy One, blessed be He! They do not know that they are brought before the tribunal both before they enter into this world and after they leave it; they are ignorant of the many reincarnations and secret works which they have to undergo, and of the number of naked souls, and how many naked spirits roam about in the other world without being able to enter within the veil of the King's Palace. Men do not know how the souls revolve like a stone that is thrown from a sling. But the time is at hand when these mysteries will be disclosed (Zohar II 99b).

Reincarnation is seen as an opportunity for the soul to achieve what it did not achieve in a previous life. It can be a time of reward for fulfilling one's mission or a time of punishment. I guess this gives us good reason to try and live an honest life this time around.

There are many Jews who are going to read this chapter and the next and see it as nonsense. That's fine—just please keep reading.

CHAPTER 19

SLIPPING INTO A PAST LIFE

There is a very good chance that what I am about to write will wind up exploding into cyberspace with one touch of the delete key. On the other hand, if this book is to have meaning, then I have to have the courage to reveal myself. So here goes.

It all began over twenty-five years ago when the respected psychotherapist Doctor Brian Weiss wrote *Many Lives Many Masters*. The book was a true story about his accidental exploration into the past life of one of his female patients and how that information was used to help her.

I read the book, every word verifying what I had always believed but never admitted. Doctor Weiss lived in Miami and consequently, I had a front row seat watching his great success as well as hearing the ridicule that emanated from the psychiatric medical community.

Brian Weiss was the rage! Over the next few years, if you knew someone who knew someone, you just might be able to get an appointment with Doctor Weiss. But if not, other psychologists and psychiatrists threw their hats into this extraordinary arena, offering hypnosis in the quest to take their patients into a past life experience.

I did not know anyone who knew Dr. Weiss, but I still became one of those subjects, anxious and willing to explore the possibilities. The first time I was ever taken into a deep hypnotic state, I remember the therapist asking me what I was seeing around me and then asking what I was wearing. I proceeded to tell her a story, one that felt very strange—real one moment and ridiculous the next.

I saw myself as a male, an American Indian. Our tribe was being attacked. We were cut off from a retreat, cliffs at our backs. Rather than give up, we ran toward the ragged precipice. Together we jumped to our death. I remember the sensation of falling, but it all happened so quickly that I really did not have time to think. It was as if I had been dropped into the middle of a movie. As I was falling, I could see my body going down and feel my soul rising up. The therapist brought me out before my body hit the ground. She was frightened. I was not.

Before this event, I was always terrified of heights. So afraid that once, when we were on a bus in the Swiss Alps and everyone got out for a better view of the magnificent vista, I had to crawl on the ground because I was too frightened to stand. After my regression, I was no longer afraid.

I could write a thousand words about what transpired over the next few years of my life as I explored the power of my own intuition. But I won't. What I do want to share with you is something incredible that happened many years later.

My husband Mel and I have a blended family of six children. I can assure you, I never told the story of my Indian regression to our children. They would have considered me wacko!

One day, Mel's oldest son Barry shared that he had participated in a past life regression—not shocking since his wife is a therapist dealing in alternative therapies, although she is not the one who hypnotized him. In his regression, Barry told his father that he was an Indian living with his tribe. Yes, you guessed it! They were attacked and Barry jumped off a cliff to his death.

Crazy? I know and hard to believe! They say that we come around with the same people, each lifetime an opportunity to make things right. I guess Barry and I still have work to do.

A few months after my first regression, I decided to try again. In that regression, I was a priest living in a monastery. When asked by the therapist to describe my surroundings, I could only describe the room where I was lying on a bed, a cell really, bare and cold. I was old and near death. (I know, first an Indian and then a priest-beyond weird.)

After this regression, an experience I had years earlier came back to me. My husband and I were on a tour in Israel. At one point, we visited the ancient monastery of St. George in *Wadi Qelt*, a sixth-century cliff-hanging complex near the Dead Sea. The entire time we were walking through the massive site, I had an overwhelming feeling that I had been there before. In fact, as we moved down the twisting ancient passageways, I remember knowing what was coming next. I anticipated the hallway filled with tiny rooms where the priests lived. I knew we were about to see the dining hall before we turned the corner. I know it sounds like I am making this up, but I can assure you it did happen. And I can also assure you that I was freaked out!

The last regression I did during that time period was the most disturbing of all. In it, I was a young woman in a concentration camp, cowering in a corner the unwilling mistress of a Nazi.

I refused to stay in that regression, pulling myself out after only a couple of minutes. I remember standing up and telling the therapist that it was ridiculous and I was finished with all the crazy stuff I had been doing!

I tried to block out the memory of that momentary experience, but it remains like a black and white photograph etched into my brain.

That brief regression had a powerful impact on my life. It helped me to understand why even as a young girl, I had an obsessive need to learn about the Holocaust. It also explains why I panic when I am riding in a car and outside gas fumes seep in. The smell overwhelms me and I feel as if I am suffocating.

Many years after this regression, I began to write *Hearts Of Fire*, the book that would eventually morph into *Clouds Across the Sun*. I knew from page one of *Hearts of Fire* that I would write about the Holocaust. It was as if I had no other choice. I think reading the summary of my book will give you insight into the impact that the regression had on my life.

Before the end of WWII, Hitler charged a group of his most trusted and brilliant comrades with a mission—educate your progeny, and then elevate them to positions of power throughout the world. Steeped in fact and impeccably researched, Clouds Across the Sun is the story of just one of these children.

From Naples, Florida, New York City and Washington D.C., to Israel and then the killing grounds of Vilnius, Poland (Lithuania), this story is one of great romance, discovery, redemption and enlightenment as Jotto Wells discovers her Jewish soul and unravels the intrigue surrounding a plan to take over the government of the United States.

Morgan is one of the characters in the book. The things that happened to her in my story were as real to me as my breath. At times, she and I were one. The day I finished *Clouds Across the Sun,* something shifted inside of me. By telling Morgan's story, I told my own story, and I was able to let it go. Although the smell of gas still terrifies me!

All of this took place over twenty years ago. Looking back, I have to admit it is a bit confusing that I was not always a Jew. I have yet to work that out in my mind.

I have not talked about any of this for years. It just got filed away in my memory. I have never written about it. And I never expected to walk that path again. But a few months ago, I put my toe back into the water when my rabbi offered to hypnotize me. I hope I have the words to describe this experience, sitting in the rabbi's office, his voice gentle in my ears.

Within minutes, I was in an alternative reality. I was a scribe hiding in a cave in Israel. I talked about the other scribes in other caves, knowing that they were all doing exactly what I was doing: copying sacred manuscripts. The Jews were under attack, and I knew that I had to complete my work quickly because it was only a matter of time before I would be discovered and killed. I worked day and night, alone, cut off from my family and friends.

Every few days, two powerfully built couriers arrived. They would shove aside the massive bolder sealing the entrance to the cave. They were there to deliver meager rations of food and water. I then gave them the parchment I had completed and they left, sealing me inside again.

I knew I was doing important work, holy work. I was willing to give my life for the words, the faith and for G-d.

This last experience touched me in ways I find hard to describe. When I wrote *And So It Was Written*, I kept trying to have my story take place in a cave in the Judean hills. I didn't know why at the time. I understand now.

Every past life reincarnation I experienced changed my life. This is my truth.

CHAPTER 20

JEWISH ANGELS? WHO KNEW?

I had always believed that angels were a symbol of Christianity. As a matter of fact, when I thought of angels, I thought of death. And so, I never bought a single card, a stuffed animal, a doll or a picture that depicted an angel. I wanted them nowhere near my children.

But a prayer we read daily confused me. *O Fashioner of ministering angels; all of Whose ministering angels stand at the summit of the universe and proclaim with awe, together, loudly the words of the living G-d and King of the universe. They are all beloved; they are all flawless; they are all mighty, they all do the will of their Maker with dread and reverence (Page 86 Artscroll),* daily *siddur*/prayerbook.

I remember clearly a conversation I had with the rabbi after I asked him to explain the prayer to me. I remember thinking, *what's with the angels?* That is obviously not how I phrased the question, but that is how the question was rolling around in my head.

"It's about the angels," he said.

"There are angels in Judaism?" I asked. I had always believed that I was protected by something, but I never gave that something a name. Now that I could, I was more than willing to claim angels for myself.

He then told me a glorious *Midrash* (story) taught in Judaism. According to our Sages, whenever you fulfill a mitzvah (a commandment), you acquire an angel. Say a kind word, give a sincere compliment, offer assistance, visit a sick friend, give charity and the angels will come to love and protect you. Conversely, commit a transgression and you will acquire an angel-accuser.

I would have let the words *angel-accuser* slip right on by, not wanting or needing an explanation, but my writing group insisted on knowing more. So I was forced to delve deeper.

First thing I learned was the word *Satan* is the Hebrew word for accuser. Satan? No way! I wanted to write about angels, and now, I was being forced to research the devil! I am a full-blown Pollyanna. I believe in goodness, my glass overflowing and the sun always shinning. I do not believe in the devil: Period, end of story.

Thank goodness, as I researched, I found myself taking a glorious sigh of relief. Judaism does not see Satan as the Christians do: a fallen angel who challenges G-d. In Judaism, Satan is merely another angel whose mission is to be obedient and subservient to G-d. We believe Satan is our evil inclination, testing us, tempting us into sin and then testifying against us in the Heavenly court when we die. That is why Satan is known as the accuser. He is also the Angel of Death charged with taking human souls from this world. There is no direct reference in the Hebrew Bible to the Angel of Death. We do, however, find many references in rabbinic literature.

Here is the important thing to remember, we do not have to bend to the will of this angel. We have free will, and we have the ability to fight all temptation.

Ok, enough. I am going to make sure I am surrounded by lots of angels. And so, I try and do good deeds and keep the bad stuff to a minimum. Sometimes, I am really good at it, and other times, not so good.

I live in Miami, and we have a lot of traffic. I mean big time traffic, the kind you see on TV and you think to yourself, I'm glad I don't live there. Only, Miami is a glorious place to live, and so you keep coming, thus the horrific traffic.

So there I was inching along on the causeway that leads from Miami Beach to the mainland. There is a tiny Fiat in the lane next to me. The girl driving is texting, hitting the brake and then texting again. I kept glancing at her. In truth, I was feeling somewhat self-righteous since I didn't happen to be looking at my phone like I do sometimes. Then, to my horror, she turned around and spoke to what was obviously a young child sitting in a car seat. She then went back to her texting.

I went from upset to furious. The cars began to move a bit faster, and she was no longer next to me. Still, we were both going in the same direction and were now in an area with traffic lights. I was a mad-woman on a mission. I kept trying to pull up next to her. I was going to give her a piece of my mind and rectify the situation. Finally, we were beside one another at a light. I motioned for her to lower her window. She did. Now, try and imagine what happened next.

"Do you love your baby?" I called from my car to hers.

She gave me the evil eye and yelled, "What are you talking about?"

"I said, "If you love your child, then put the phone down before you both get killed!" (Don't you think that should have brought a good angel to my side?)

She shot me a dirty look and a middle finger. What came out of my mouth next mortified even me. She screamed something back as her window went up.

I can assure you, that any good angels that were coming my way were shoved aside by the angel accuser. This story does not make me proud. In fact, it made me ashamed of myself. I tell you this because even when I try really hard to do nice things, sometimes it backfires. You can be sure, I will continue to call in the angels and bully away those bad guys. And along the way, I hope I will learn to control my temper and my mouth.

CHAPTER 21

WHO ARE THESE ANGELS?

After my conversation with the rabbi, I had lots of questions about angels: Who are they, and what are their jobs? Angels are defined as metaphysical beings—messengers of G-d. They are spiritual, but they have no free will. They can only do exactly what they have been commanded to do by their Creator. In our medieval rabbinic literature, it is said that every human being is assigned an angel (Pesikta Rabbati 44:8).

It is written that the Jewish soul surpasses that of the angel. The reason: angels have no free will. They do as they are instructed by G-d. Conversely, we do have freedom of choice. When we perform a *mitzvah* (a good deed/commandment), it is of greater value than that of the angels, because we made the *decision* to act as G-d commanded.

According to Maimonides, the great *Sephardic Torah* scholar who lived from 1138-1204, angels have certain tasks. Some are dispatched on missions of kindness, and some are sent to heal. Some angels are even created by G-d as a result of our actions. I guess that means if we do something really fabulous, angels can actually be created.

I can't help but think about September 11, 2001. When the heroic firefighters and police officers ran into those burning towers. I know they created angels that carried them into heaven.

Whenever I hear the word angel, I immediately imagine a human form with wings. In fact, that is a description in *Exodus* 25:20 when the Jews are told how to make the Ark that will hold the Ten Commandments. *The (angel) shall have their wings spread upwards, shielding the ark cover with their wings, with their faces toward one another; [turned] toward the ark cover shall be the faces of the cherubim (Exodus 25:20).*

There are many other examples when angels are given a human form. We are taught that in this way, we are able to conceive the essence of angels. It is much the same when the *Torah* describes G-d as having a *strong hand and outstretched arm.* G-d does not have an arm. This is said so we may begin to comprehend G-d's might.

When you read the words *heavenly court* in the prayer book, it is referring to the heavenly court of angels. G-d makes the plans, and His angels carry them out. That is their job. Read the following line once, and then let it sit with you for a moment. *One thousand angels will sit at our Judgment Day. We need **only one** to vote for us to **avoid** punishment. They must all be unanimous to convict.*

Even though I don't like the thought of punishment, it is said there are angels charged with executing G-d's severe judgment. Severe judgment makes me cringe.

What must we do to become a better Jew and avoid God's severe judgment? Even the most religious people I have met feel they should and could be better Jews?

In the *Shema* Prayer: *Hear, (listen) Israel, the LORD is our G-d, the LORD is One* we are commanded by G-d to listen. It makes great sense to me that our first step towards being a better Jew is the willingness to listen and hear. So, the next time an angel whispers in my ear that I need to be kinder, more generous, more empathetic to others and less judgmental, I intend to listen!

In *HaTorah* 2:7, it is noted that there are ten levels of angels based on the angel's comprehension of G-d. Until Maimonides, these varieties of angels were not described. It was believed we lacked a vocabulary able to define them.

CHAPTER 22

MEET THE ANGELS

I know what comes next might be pushing the envelope a bit. A few minutes ago, you may not have even known there were Jewish angels. Now I am telling you there are different levels of angels.

I actually did not intend to list Maimonides' descriptions of the angels and their ranks, but I have to confess, I am a big fan of the man. Maimonides was a twelfth century sage and the first person to write a systematic code of all Jewish law known as the *Mishneh Torah*: fourteen books written one thousand years after the *Mishnah* we find in the *Talmud*. Please note the difference in these two books. One is the *Mishneh* and the other *Mishnah*.

Maimonides also wrote one of the greatest philosophic writings on Judaism: *The Guide to the Perplexed*. He was a physician to the sultan of Egypt and wrote numerous books on medicine. He also served as the leader of Cairo's Jewish community.

Here goes my simplified version of Maimonides' descriptions of angels and their ranks:

Chayos: Created to be G-d supporters. They are the highest level of angels. They are known for their great enlightenment.

Ophanim: They never sleep. They are prepared for action and guard G-d's throne in heaven.

Areilim: Known for courage and understanding.

Chashmallim: Known for their love, kindness and grace.

Seraphim: Known for justice.

Malakhim: Known for their beauty and mercy.

Elokim: Commitment to the victory of good over evil.

Beni Elohim: Child-like, represent the pure ideals of transformation.

Cherubim: Known for helping people deal with sin that separates them from G-d so they can draw closer.

Ishim: Rank of angel closest to the level of human beings. Here to build G-d's kingdom on Earth.

Rabbi Gunther Plaut, a modern day Reform rabbi of blessed memory, wrote the following. Allow me to paraphrase: "In the Hebrew Bible, angels speak, sit, stand, walk and climb ladders. They fly, ride horses, use weapons and escort people to heaven. They bring prophecy, dialogue with G-d and act as G-d's cabinet—as a sounding board and in advisory roles. The angels worship G-d and sing in G-d's heavenly choir. They do G-d's bidding, record our deeds in the Book of Life, carry divine messages and act as heavenly janitors and security guards.

Other angels lift peoples' spirits and help people in time of need. They serve as G-d's escort service to heavenly realms and even to death."

Here is a lovely *Midrash* (story): *No blade of grass grows without an angel telling it to grow. It is the Jewish belief that everything on earth has a spiritual counterpart—even a blade of grass has an angel insuring that it obtains nourishment and dies at its appointed time.*

My prayer for you is that you will always be surrounded by *mitzvah* angels.

CHAPTER 23

WHISPERS FROM ANGELS

I told you that I never believed in angels. Yet, I always believed that we could be contacted with messages from G-d, if only we would open our eyes and our hearts. To that end, I want to share some of my stories with you.

My mother-in law Rose passed away many years ago. She lived in Florida but wanted to be buried beside her husband in New Jersey. We were standing beside the grave; the air was crisp and the sky cloudy. A bumblebee circled my husband's head and then mine. We looked at each other and smiled. Rose was like a bumblebee, prickly on the outside but sweet as honey on the inside.

After the internment, our children piled into a car to go to the house where my husband grew up and to see the schools he attended. When the kids returned, my daughter said, *"Mom, we had the weirdest thing happen. We had a bumblebee in the car, and we couldn't get it out!"*

The next day my husband, my sister-in-law Eileen and I went to a local diner for breakfast. We walked to a booth in the very back of the restaurant. When we sat down, Mel pointed to his sister. Perched on her shoulder was a bumblebee.

Was Rose trying to communicate with us, to let us know she was okay and would watch over us? Darn right she was!

Making a new friend

How does that happen? I hope after reading my next story, you might pause, and the next time you meet someone you like, instead of walking away, reach out.

The year was 1986, and I was on a young woman's mission to Israel, sponsored by the Miami Jewish Federation. On that trip, I was given the opportunity to meet with politicians and various men and women who were instrumental in helping settle the State of Israel.

I had the honor of hearing a presentation by Menachem Perlmutter—known as the architect of the Negev. He was one of the men who invented drip irrigation, the watering system that turned the Negev desert into the breadbasket of Europe.

Menachem was six feet four inches tall with blond hair and piercing blue eyes. He was a dynamic speaker, holding the audience spellbound as he shared the story of his life. We traversed time as he told us what it was like coming to Israel, becoming an engineer and fighting in every war to secure a Jewish homeland.

At the end of his talk, he rolled up the sleeve of his shirt, and showed the audience the number tattooed on his arm. A collective gasp was heard, and then an eerie hush fell over the three hundred people in attendance. He then spoke of losing his entire family to the gas chambers, everyone but his beloved older brother. Wiping tears from my eyes, I knew I had to meet this man. I stood in line waiting for my turn.

As I stood in front of him, staring into his kindly eyes, I said, *"Mr. Perlmutter, you touched me deeply. May I have your card so that I can write to you?"*

"I would like that," he replied.

At the time, I had no idea how this moment would impact my life. Hundreds of letters followed. His correspondence covered the marriages of his two daughters, the births of his grandchildren, celebrations and joy, wars and sadness. Pride and sometimes angst dripped from his words, words not always easy to decipher. Menachem refused to use a typewriter, and his writing was often almost illegible. As for the later years, he would have no part in e-mail or using a computer!

Menachem came to America every year representing the Jewish National Fund. My husband and I always tried to meet him. We also went to Israel, and he hosted us in his home. One brief encounter and a determined decision began a twenty-five year friendship that changed my life forever.

Despite being in Aushwitz at sixteen and suffering the loss of his beloved family, Menachem still believed in G-d and in the goodness of humanity.

Menachem told me this story. While in the Auschwitz, for entertainment, the Nazis would line people up in front of a freshly dug pit. They Jews were ordered to jump across. If they made it, they lived. If not, they fell into the pit and were shot. In line with Menachem, was a frail old rabbi. Menachem asked, *"Aren't you afraid?"*

The rabbi looked at him and smiled. *"No, my son. I am not afraid. I will jump on the back of G-d."*

The rabbi made it across. Perhaps that is why Menachem never tried to explain to me why he believed in G-d. He just did. Through his example, he fortified my faith.

I lost Menachem Perlmutter three years ago. A week after he died, I went to Denver, Colorado to speak at a Jewish art and book fair. When I arrived at the venue, I was handed a note with the name of the room I would be speaking in.

I opened the card. I was to speak in the Perlmutter room. A coincidence? Not in my mind. Not a chance. Menachem was telling me he was there.

CHAPTER 24

EVERY MOMENT IS CONNECTED TO THE NEXT

To me, this next story goes even deeper than all the rest. The reason is the convoluted circumstances that brought about what I see as a miracle.

One evening while speaking to a book club, I met a professor from the University of Miami, Anita Meinbach. We had an instant connection and have become close friends.

Anita heads a Jewish foundation and has ties with the Holocaust community. She spoke to me one day about Rubin Offenbach, a survivor who had recently lost his beloved wife. I asked Anita if she would introduce me to Rubin so I could interview him. To this day, I do not know why. I never intended to write another Holocaust novel, and I had no idea what I would do with the information I got from the interview.

Still, I made an appointment and hours of interviews followed. Rubin transported me into the darkness. His ability and willingness to recall agonizing details and even dates were astounding. Brave beyond comprehension, Rubin spoke often to non-Jewish high school kids. He told me: *I don't think they understand. I don't think I reach them.*

He gave me copies of documents his daughter, a lawyer, had secured from concentration camp records. The Nazis kept impeccable records, and reading them made me sick to my stomach!

Each time I went, there was a *tallit* bag sitting on a chair next to the table. I asked him if he went to synagogue. He looked at me and sighed. I paraphrase: *"I go to show my respect. What I believe? I don't know."*

Rubin had a gentle demeanor, but I could see that behind that persona was a powerful and determined man. As an immigrant and a survivor of the Holocaust, he came to America with nothing. His first job was a dishwasher in a restaurant on Miami Beach. He went on to become a very successful businessman.

He and his wife raised four daughters. Only one still lived in Miami. He was proud of his family. He showed me family photos and shared some stories of his life. I was deeply touched by his honesty, but the entire time I kept asking myself: *What was I doing and why?*

One day, I called just to say hello to Rubin. I had not talked to him for weeks. His daughter answered. Sadly, she told me her father had passed away, and the funeral would be the following day. I was unable to attend, but I was determined to show my respect for this amazing man.

I went to the house to make a *shiva* call. I walked into the home of his youngest daughter in late afternoon. I introduced myself. They knew who I was, because their father had spoken to them about the writer who was interviewing him.

The lawyer from California and her husband had just come back from a run, and the grandchildren were sprawled about the living room. As if by some unspoken word, within minutes, I was sitting with Rubin's four daughters at the dining room table. Everyone else had quietly disappeared.

An hour later, I was still there. The girls openly shared stories about being raised by parents who were survivors. They were proud that their mother always had food cooked and ready to be served to all their friends, anytime, day or night.

Eventually talk turned to spirituality. Only the youngest daughter had a connection to Judaism. I told the girls the bumblebee story. I said, *"Just stay vigilant, keep your eyes and hearts open. You never know how your father might reach out to you."*

Even though most of the family was ambivalent about Judaism, out of love for their father, they were all going to Friday night services at Temple Judea in Coral Gables to say the *Kaddish* prayer. When I finally left, it was with hugs, a few tears and a promise to stay in touch.

The family went to synagogue that night. My husband and I are not members, but ten years earlier, we had donated ONE book in honor of our friend who became the first woman president of the synagogue. Temple Judea has close to two thousand members and at least one thousand *Siddurs* (prayer books).

During the service, Rubin's son-in-law turned to the front of the prayer book.

The inscription read: **Donated by Ellen and Mel Brazer.**

They immediately sent me a text message with a photograph of the inside cover.

Rubin had reached out to his children. By sending me the photograph, I knew the message had been heard. I also knew exactly why I was destined to meet Rubin Offenbach!

CHAPTER 25

COME MEET SOME PROPHETS

The Hebrew Bible begins with the *Torah*—the five books of Moses: *Genesis, Exodus, Leviticus, Numbers* and *Deuteronomy*. I know I have repeated myself again, but I have a theory. I believe if we read something enough times, we just might remember it. This is going to be news to many of you. It was to me! Jews do not *ever* refer to the Hebrew Bible as the Old Testament. That is strictly a Christian designation. It is a Christian way of setting The Hebrew Bible apart from the New Testament bible. (The New Testament covers the birth of Jesus through the death of the last apostle). So, when you are looking up information on the Internet, and you see the words *Old Testament*, you are not on a Jewish website.

So here we go. The Hebrew Bible, *Tanakh,* is not **one** book but a compilation of **twenty-four** books. The word *Tanakh* is an acronym (contraction) derived from Hebrew letters that stand for *Torah, Prophets* and the *Writings*. Ah hah! That sounds so simple: The Hebrew Bible is *Torah, Prophets* and the *Writings*.

The longer I go to classes and study, the more I realize the need to know the Hebrew names for the Five Books of Moses. The reason: You may never hear a Conservative or Orthodox rabbi refer to the Books in English.

Genesis/Bereishit (In the beginning).
Exodus/Shemot (The names).
Leviticus/ Vayikra (And He called).
Numbers/Bamidbar (In the wilderness).
Deuteronomy/ Davarim (The words).

The next books in the Hebrew Bible, after the Five Books of Moses, are the eight books of the Prophets (*Nevi'im*): *Joshua, Judges, I-II Samuel, I-II Kings, Isaiah, Jeremiah and Ezekiel*. The final Twelve Minor Prophets are all grouped together in one book. Since I will not be delving into their lives, I will leave out the names for you to look up for yourself.

The last books in the Bible are the Writings (*K'tuvim*). They include *Psalms, Proverbs, Job, Song of Songs, Ruth, Lamentations, Ecclesiastes, Esther, Daniel, Ezra, Nehemiah, I-II Chronicles.*

What is a prophet? Simply stated, a person who sees the future. These prophets were known to have had the gift of prophecy. Okay, I know that is pretty obvious, but every once in a while, it is fun to have something so obvious. In ancient times, the prophets were seen as representatives chosen by G-d to speak to the people.

Let's begin with the **Book of *Joshua***. All I ever knew about Joshua was from the song: *Joshua fought the battle of Jericho and the walls came tumbling down!* I never knew Joshua was Moses' successor, or that he was the one to lead our people into the Land of Israel. Joshua was also given the responsibility to pass on the Oral Law after receiving it directly from Moses. I hope you are smiling because you just heard a reference to the Oral Law, and you know what that is.

The Book of *Joshua* is about Joshua's ultimatums to the numerous kings of the land of Canaan (Lebanon, Syria, Jordan and Israel)—as he claimed the Promised Land for the Jews.

Joshua gave these kings options: evacuate, remain and make peace or go to war. Only one tribe left peacefully, and only one tribe asked for peace. The rest prepared for war with the Jews. The book of *Joshua* is about battles, spies and miraculous victories.

We learn when it came time for the Jews to cross the Jordan River with the Holy Ark, G-d intervened. The water flowed away, leaving the riverbed dry for the Jews to cross. Once across, the waters flowed again.

In this book, we have an angel, one who rebuked Joshua for neglecting to study *Torah*, while at war with Jericho. His face to the ground, Joshua prayed for forgiveness. After beseeching G-d's compassion, Joshua commanded the Jews to always find the time and the place to study *Torah*, regardless of their circumstances.

We read about Joshua's farewell speech before his death. He was one hundred and ten years old when he made a covenant with the people, yet again reminding them to always observe the *Torah* and the Commandments. He is buried in Mount Ephraim in Israel.

I know this age thing, *how long they lived,* is hard for us to comprehend. Perhaps they recorded time differently in ancient days? Or perhaps, G-d gave them that many years. You can embrace these numbers, they are throughout the Bible, or disregard them. I am not sure it matters.

CHAPTER 26

THE LADY JUDGE

The next book in the Prophets is *Judges*. This book covers the period after Joshua's death. The underlying theme in *Judges* and throughout the Hebrew Bible is that when the Jews do not keep their covenant with G-d, the results are catastrophic.

I know, I know. Who wants to hear or even think about that? I certainly would like to believe it is not true! But when you look at the history of the Jews—we have had one heck of a turbulent ride throughout our history. Is it possible that G-d is angry with us for not keeping our covenant with Him? Our sages teach that our covenant is not just about our relationship with G-d, but it is also about our relationship with our fellow Jews and with all of humanity.

The book of *Judges* covers a period of three hundred and sixty-five years. During those years, there were seventeen judges. These Judges were the Jewish leaders. Their goal was to unify our people and deal with spiritual, legal and military matters. I will only write about two of the Judges, Deborah and Samson.

Deborah, one of our first Judges was a woman! Considering that for thousands of years, a Jewish woman's role was strictly defined as taking care of the family, home and insuring that the Jewish traditions were carried forward—a female judge seems a huge contradiction.

Deborah was known to be G-d fearing and to have great wisdom and empathy. It is said that she counseled fairly and the people flocked to her for advice.

Many of the attributes that made Deborah so great were indeed female characteristics. But there was another side to this complicated woman. She was a fearless warrior with outspoken convictions.

Deborah prophesied that the mighty Canaanite general, Sisera, a man who had oppressed the Jewish people for over twenty years, would fall at the hands of a Jewish army. To insure that prophecy was carried out, Deborah ordered her commander Barak, the most influential man in Israel, to raise an army of ten thousand men to defeat Sisera.

Go! This is the day the LORD has given Sisera into your hands. Has not the LORD gone ahead of you (Judges 4:14)?

Barak resisted taking his army to war against the iron chariots and cavalry of Sisera without the warrior prophetess, Deborah by his side. Deborah was pragmatic. She warned Barak that if she accompanied him the victory would not be his, but instead, the victory of a woman. Barak still insisted Deborah be at his side.

What Deborah had foreseen came to fruition. There were great battles and miraculous victories for the Jews. Interestingly, the infamous Canaanite general, Sisera did not meet his demise while in battle. Instead, a woman named Jael murdered Sisera while he slept.

From this great epic story emerges the *Song of Deborah* (Judges 5:2-31), a victory chant sung by Deborah and Barak that describes their final battle.

The story of Deborah the Judge ended with the statement: *After the battle, there was peace in the land for forty years* (Judges 5:31).

Many think of Deborah as the mother of Israel.

In my opinion, during my lifetime, there lived another mother of Israel, and her name was Golda Meir. In 1969, at the age of sixty-nine, Golda became the fourth Prime Minister of the state of Israel. This plain looking lady, who wore no make-up and owned no fancy clothing, had the confidence and determination to sit with the icons of American Jewish society. She never held back, insisting that the State of Israel must survive! She did this with aplomb and determination, as she single-handedly raised millions of dollars for the struggling State. She was a Zionist, a diplomat and a warrior woman. She died at eighty years old from leukemia.

I remember strolling through the tree-lined paths of the Mount Herzl National Cemetery in Jerusalem. Approaching her gravesite, I walked up the three steps that led to her monument. There was a bed of flowers blooming to my left. No flowers were set upon her grave, only rocks, as is our tradition. I read many different teachings as to why we place a rock on a Jewish grave. The one that resonated with me was that flowers will wither and die, a rock will remain forever.

I stared at her Hebrew name carved into the black granite and wept, overcome by grief. Golda had been a touchstone in my life, whenever I felt inadequate, unworthy or overwhelmed, I would think about Golda.

And so, standing at her grave, I wept. I want to share this quote from Golda, one I think about every time Israel is embroiled in a conflict.

*We can forgive the Arabs for killing our children. We **cannot** forgive them for forcing us to kill their children. We will only have peace with the Arabs when they love their children more than they hate us.*

CHAPTER 27

SAMSON: THE ORIGINAL SUPER HERO

An angel of G-d appeared before Zealphonis, a childless woman. The angel told Zealphonis she would conceive a son, a boy who would one day save Israel from their hated oppressors, the Philistines. The Philistines had terrorized the Jewish people for forty long and bitter years. She was also told that her son was to be raised as a *Nazarite,* consecrated to serve G-d—meaning he could never drink wine, cut his hair or touch a dead body. She named her son Samson.

As an adult, Samson decided to marry a Philistine woman, despite his parents' disapproval. Why Samson would align himself with the enemy by marrying a non-Jew is beyond me!

As he walked in the vineyards to claim his bride, a lion attacked Samson. Samson tore the lion apart with his bare hands, realizing for the first time his incalculable strength.

Thirty Philistine men joined the seven-day wedding feast. During the festivities, Samson offered a riddle to the men, promising each one a set of the finest linen clothing if they could come up with the answer to the riddle. If they could not, then they would have to give Samson new clothing. The riddle was based on Samson returning to the carcass of the lion he had slain. Inside the carcass, he found a bee comb.

Unable to figure out the riddle, the men threatened Samson's wife, telling her they would burn her father's house to the ground unless she got her husband to reveal the answer.

Samson's wife begged and begged until he finally relented and told her the answer. She then revealed the answer to the Philistine men. They went to Samson and said: *What is sweeter than honey? And what is stronger than a lion?* (Judges 14:18)

At that moment, Samson knew his wife had betrayed him. He fled in fury. Seeking retribution, he murdered thirty Philistine men, took their clothing and sent them to the men who had answered the riddle.

Many months later, Samson returned to his wife. When he tried to go into her bedchamber he was forbidden. That is when he found out that his wife was no longer his wife. Her father had given her to another man.

Blinded by rage, Samson vowed revenge. What follows is a bit hard to envision. Samson caught three hundred foxes, tied their tails together and put a flaming torch between each pair of tails. He led the foxes into the fields where they burned the Philistine crops to the ground. When the Philistines learned why Samson had burned their fields, in retaliation, they burned Samson's wife and her father alive.

Beware of revenge

After his wife's death, Samson became a vigilante—using his immense strength to kill Philistines at every opportunity! His incredible victories convinced the Jewish people that Samson had been chosen by G-d to lead them. He was appointed as Judge, the thirteenth in Israel since Joshua. During his years as a Judge of Israel, Samson continued to perform miraculous feats of strength.

Samson married a second Philistine woman, Delilah, after she converted to Judaism. The Philistines were desperate to capture Samson, and they saw Delilah as their chance. They offered Delilah a fortune in silver if she could entice Samson to tell her where his great strength came from. Again, Samson fell under the deceitful charms of a woman.

Samson said: *A razor has never come to my head; for I have been a Nazarite unto God from my mother's womb. If I be shaven, then my strength will go from me, and I shall become weak, and be like any other man* (Judges16: 17).

As he slept, Delilah had Samson's hair shaved off. The Philistines captured Samson. They blinded him and threw him into prison. Eventually, Samson was taken for a public execution. The execution was held in a pagan temple filled to overflowing with Philistines who had come to watch the great Samson die.

Ah, but his captors were not too smart. Samson had been in prison a long time—long enough for his hair to have grown back! As he stood between two columns, he said: *My LORD, G-d! Remember me and strengthen me just this one time, O G-d, and I will extract vengeance from the Philistines for one of my two eyes. Let my soul die with the Philistines* (Judges 16:28-30)!

Samson dislodged the columns holding up the temple, and all the people standing within the structure were crushed including Samson. In Judges, it is said, Samson killed more Philistines in this last act of great courage than he killed in all the wars he had previously fought.

CHAPTER 28

A LESSON TO LEARN

The Books of Samuel I and II are the next set of books in the Hebrew Bible under the *Prophets*. They were written by Samuel, the last Judge.

Samuel was the son of Hannah, another barren woman who begged G-d to give her a child. Hannah vowed that when she gave birth, she would dedicate her son to the LORD.

Hannah gave birth to a son, and she named him Samuel. While Samuel was still a small boy, Hannah took him to Shiloh—the religious center of Israel where the Tabernacle holding the Ten Commandments was located. Keeping her commitment, Hannah turned her only child over to the care of the High Priest of Israel, Eli, the only man allowed to enter the Tabernacle.

Under Eli's tutelage, Samuel became a deeply religious young man. The story of Samuel's life takes us onto the battlefield with the Philistines at Aphek. (Yes, the Philistines again.) In that battle, the Jews lost four thousand men.

Refusing to succumb to defeat by the Philistines, Eli's two sons demanded that their father allow them to take the Ark of the Covenant into battle with them. The brothers believed that if the Ark were carried

THE WONDERING JEW: MY JOURNEY INTO JUDAISM

at the front of their army's advance, it would protect them—just as it had in the time of Joshua.

The result was disastrous; the Jews were slaughtered: Thirty thousand died, including Eli's two sons. To compound that catastrophe, the Tabernacle holding the Ten Commandments fell into the hands of the Philistines!

When Eli learned that the Ark was lost and that his sons had died, he was so overcome with grief, he died. He was ninety-eight years old and had judged the Jews for forty years.

Samuel became Eli's successor as a Judge of the Jewish people. In the Book of *Samuel,* we read about the horrid calamities that G-d rained down upon the Philistines for stealing the Ark of the Covenant. We follow all that transpired before the Philistines finally agreed to return the Holy Ark to the Jews.

More wars ensued even after they returned the Ark, but eventually *the Philistines were humbled and did not invade the territory of Israel again* (Samuel 8:14).

Samuel was beloved by the people, and he is seen as one of the most important Judges in our history. Ruling into old age, Samuel grew tired. He turned to his two sons for assistance, appointing them Judges. But sadly, his sons were corrupt, taking bribes and perverting justice.

The elders of Israel gathered and came to Samuel. *"Behold, thou art old, and thy sons walk not in your ways; now make us a king to judge us like all the nations* (Samuel, 8:5).

At this point in the history of the Jewish people, we had Prophets and Judges but never a king! Believing that the only King of the Jews was G-d, at first Samuel refused to appoint a king—but the elders were relentless.

Eventually the LORD instructed Samuel: *Heed their demands and appoint a king for them (Samuel 8:22).* As an aside, Moses had prophesied that the Jews would eventually appoint a king of G-d's choosing.

- 95 -

I am searching hard to find the messages in these Bible stories about the lives of our forefathers. I know that the ancient rabbinic scholars took one sentence, looked for meaning, and then wrote pages and pages of opinions.

I am more of a big picture person. Both Eli and Samuel were selected by G-d and given enormous responsibility: Eli to be the High Priest of Israel and Samuel to be a Judge. And yet, these men had fathered and raised sons who were great disappointments.

I think this story has a message for all of us. Our children are their own people, with their own paths to walk and their own mistakes to make in this life.

But I did not always believe or know that. I really thought I could control my children! Of course, like most of us, I learned that was not going to happen the minute they hit their teenage years.

At one point, we had three teenage children in our home. I was convinced that each one had fallen down a rabbit hole and climbed out as an alien from another planet. Otherwise, why had I suddenly become the enemy, someone to sneak around and hide from? When I was a teenager, I gave my parents fits! But when I became the parent, it was a shock that rocked my world.

I remember reading a poem during those chaotic years by Kahlil Gibran. The poem appeared in his book, *The Prophet* (no pun intended). The book was published in 1923, and yet it has never lost its power to reach across time. I am really honored to share it with you.

On children
Your children are not your children.
They are the sons and daughters of Life's longing for itself.
They come through you but not from you,
And though they are with you yet they belong not to you.

You may give them your love but not your thoughts,
For they have their own thoughts.
You may house their bodies but not their souls,
For their souls dwell in the house of tomorrow,
which you cannot visit, not even in your dreams.
You may strive to be like them,
but seek not to make them like you.
For life goes not backward, nor tarries with yesterday.
You are the bows from which your children
as living arrows are sent forth.
The archer sees the mark upon the path of the infinite,
and He bends you with His might
that His arrows may go swift and far.
Let your bending in the archer's hand be for gladness;
For even as He loves the arrow that flies,
so He loves also the bow that is stable.

CHAPTER 29

HERE COME THE KINGS

I want to take a breath here and tell you that I am working really hard not to confuse you or confuse myself. But *oy veh*, I am so bewildered. The books of *Samuel* are supposed to be about the Judges. And yet, the end of *Samuel II* follows the lives of King Saul and King David. Sorry, but I have no idea why the story of the first two Jewish kings are not in the Book of *Kings*! I needed to *kvetch*. It is what I do when I get frustrated.

Time to learn about the first king of Israel.

Let's imagine ourselves in the year 884 BCE, four hundred years after we arrived in the Promised Land. According to the *Talmud*, during this time period, there was an incalculable number of prophets (seers) gifted with the ability to see what others could not see. Do not confuse this ability with witchcraft, as witchcraft was forbidden.

A young man named Saul went in search of his father's lost donkeys. He traversed the entire territory looking for them. Desperate, he entered a town hoping to meet Judge Samuel—the greatest seer of his time. Saul was convinced that Judge Samuel would surely know where to find his father's donkeys.

The day before Saul arrived, the LORD had revealed to Judge Samuel that a young man was coming to him that would become the ruler of Israel. As soon as Saul approached Judge Samuel, the LORD declared: *This is the man that I told you would govern My people* (Samuel 9:18).

Judge Samuel immediately told Saul where he could find his donkeys. He then informed Saul that he had been chosen, and that one day he would become the king of Israel. Hand to heart, I am not making this up. That is how it happened.

As Saul grew to adulthood, it was obvious that he was a righteous, humble and scholarly man of integrity. But leadership required more than that—it required strength of personality, ambition and determination. Unfortunately, the future King of the Jews, Saul lacked those attributes.

The Jews had known relative peace under Judge Samuel's guidance. But now, under the rule of King Saul, the Jews were being threatened by their archenemies, the Amalekites. The Amalekites were the people who had attacked the weakest Jews as they fled from Egypt. They were a Nomadic nation. They lived on the peninsula of the Sinai in the wilderness between the southern hills of Israel and the border of Egypt. For generations, the Jews had been waiting for an opportunity to *blot out the memory of Amalek from under heaven (Deuteronomy 25: 19)*.

Judge Samuel was King Saul's mentor and guide. He relayed the LORD'S instructions: *Now go, attack Amalek, and proscribe (disallow) all that belongs to him. Spare no one; kill alike men and women, infants and suckling, oxen and sheep, camels and asses! (Samuel I, 15:3)*

King Saul took two hundred and ten thousand men and destroyed the Amalek. But King Saul made a critical mistake. He did not listen to the instructions given to him by G-d through the words of Judge Samuel. Instead, King Saul spared the Amalek leader, King Agag. He also saved the Amalekites sheep, oxen, lamb and all else of value.

King Saul had ruled over Israel for only two years when Judge Samuel confronted him and said: *For you have rejected the LORD'S command and the LORD has rejected you from being king over Israel. . .* (1 Samuel 15:17).

Judge Samuel informed King Saul that he would no longer be the king of Israel. His obligation to King Saul now complete, Judge Samuel confronted and captured the ruler of the Amalek, King Agag.

As your sword has bereaved women, so shall your mother be bereaved among women (I Samuel 15:33). Judge Samuel then fulfilled God's command and killed Agag.

In this chapter, I know I have quoted many lines from the Bible. I am enthralled by the magnificent use of language. When it is said so perfectly, I find little reason to change the words.

After reading the description surrounding King Saul's gruesome demise, I have decided to take a pass on writing the details. Regardless, it is hard to disregard the obvious theme in this chapter and in so many others: reward and punishment. Disobey

G-d, and there will be consequences.

On another front, I find it very difficult to think of a forgiving G-d as one who called for the total annihilation of a people without reason. In trying to make sense of this, I decided to look at the symbolism. I found a message. This is my interpretation, but as with anything else in the Bible, it is open to various other interpretations. G-d instructed the *total* eradication of the Amalek because their ideology called for the *total* extermination of the Jewish nation.

Because of King Saul's disobedience, King Agag survived long enough after the annihilation of his army to have fathered children. Some say Agag's DNA has been passed down through the millennium. That evil strain has presented itself over and over again: in Spain, Eastern Europe, in the Nazis, ISIS, Islamic fundamentalism and Hamas! And the list goes on.

CHAPTER 30

DAVID THE GIANT SLAYER

While King Saul was still alive, the LORD instructed Judge Samuel to go to Bethlehem, where the next king of Israel was residing with his father, Jesse. Not knowing which of Jesse's eight sons was to be king, Judge Samuel met with each one separately. When he met the youngest son, David, *ruddy-cheeked, bright-eyed and handsome,* (I Samuel 16:12.) Samuel knew that he had found the next king.

Judge Samuel anointed David in front of his family. It was not to declare David the king, but to designate that he would be next in line. *And the spirit of the LORD gripped David from that day on* (Samuel 17:13).

We now switch back to King Saul, who had fallen out of G-d's favor. *Now the spirit of the LORD had departed from Saul, and an evil spirit from the LORD began to terrify him* (I Samuel 16:1).

King Saul had become unbalanced and suspicious of everyone around him. Desperate for some solace, when he was told about a boy who played the harp brilliantly and had a melodious voice, he sent for him. It was David. King Saul had no idea that David had been anointed as the next king of Israel.

David, too young to be a soldier, shuttled between singing for King Saul and shepherding his father's flock. One day, David was sent by his father to bring food to his brothers on the battlefield as they fought the Philistines.

The Philistines had a soldier, mammoth in size and strength. His name was Goliath. The giant had set forth a challenge to the Jews: *Choose yourself a man and let him come down to me! If he can fight me and kill me, we will be slaves to you; if I defeat him and kill him, you will be slaves to us and serve us (I Samuel 17:8-9).*

Sadly, the Jews had no soldier willing to face the fearsome Goliath. When David heard about Goliath's challenge, he became enraged and stepped forward. David was offered armor and weapons but he refused. Instead, David faced the armored giant with only his slingshot and a rock. He felled Goliath, then took the giant's sword and cut off his head.

After David slew Goliath, the Jews defeated the Philistines. The result: David became a hero to the Jewish people. As a reward, he was given King Saul's daughter as a wife. Because of what happened next, I am going to assume that this marriage was not consummated for quite a while.

David and King Saul's son and heir, Jonathan, had become inseparable friends. The Bible speaks of their love for each other. I will not go into the innuendos that surround that relationship, other than to say, it appeared they were more than just friends.

King Saul, neurotic and delusional, feared the relationship between David and Jonathan—convinced that his son and David were plotting against him. *It happened the next day that Saul was overcome by a spirit of melancholy. ... and he raved incoherently in the house. David was playing [the harp]...and a spear was in Saul's hand. Then Saul threw the spear (at David) . . .But David eluded him twice (I Samuel 18:8-11).*

David fled. Hunted by King Saul's men, David was forced to hide in the land held by the Philistines. I find it hard to fathom that the future king of Israel went to live with Israel's archenemy. But it gets worse. In trade for the Philistines giving David a town where he and his men could live in safety, David became a mercenary for the Philistines.

The Philistines planned yet another attack on Israel. They questioned David's loyalty and discharged him from their army. That conflict took a gruesome toll. Israel was defeated and King Saul and his sons, including Jonathan, were killed.

David was devastated and inconsolable at the death of his beloved Jonathan. He fled the land of the Philistines and returned to Judah in the southern region that included Jerusalem. David was greeted with jubilation! The Jews had their new king.

The good years

David's forty-year reign was seen as a golden era. He subdued the Philistine threat and captured Jerusalem from the Canaanites. The Canaanites were the people inhabiting Israel when the Jews entered the Promised Land.

David declared Jerusalem the capital of Israel: ours for the first time in the four hundred forty years that we had lived in the Land of Israel.

Allow me to get a bit political for a moment. Mount Moriah, in Jerusalem, is the sacred place where Abraham offered his son Isaac to G-d and where Jacob dreamt of a ladder going up to heaven. This sacred ground is where the First and Second Temples once stood.

It is our land. We know this because we have proof that King David purchased Mount Moriah from its owner. It is recorded in the Bible in two places (II Samuel 24:24 and I Chronicles 21:25).

Today the mosque, known as the Dome of the Rock, stands on Mount Mariah. Israel allows Muslims full access to the site. Conversely, when the Muslims controlled Jerusalem, they would not allow Jews access to the Western Wall (Kotel) that stands beneath the Dome of the Rock.

Yet, for the last sixty-eight years, the world (including the United States) has **refused** to recognize Jerusalem as the capital of Israel.

It felt good to get that off my chest. I will get off my soapbox now!

King David brought the Holy Ark of the Covenant to Jerusalem. It was his intention to build a *House where G-d would dwell.*

According to *Chronicles* 1 22:7-10 King David was denied that right: *But the word of G-d was upon me, saying: 'You have shed much blood, and you have waged great wars; you shall not build a house in My Name because you have shed much blood to the ground before Me. Behold a son will be born to you. He will be a man of peace, and I shall give him peace from all his enemies around about . . . He shall build a House in My Name.*

You may have heard the story of David and Bathsheba. It is one of the most misread stories in the Bible. (Of course, first we would have to read it before it can be misread).

It is said that Bathsheba *was magnificent to gaze upon*, and when King David saw her for the first time he was smitten. Unfortunately, there was a very significant problem: Bathsheba was married to one of David's most trusted generals.

Knowing that Bathsheba's husband was engaged in battle, David sent for her. As a result, Bathsheba became pregnant. When her husband finally returned from war, David, not willing to give up Bathsheba, sent her husband back to the front lines where he was killed. David then married Bathsheba.

The prophet Nathan was sent by G-d to King David. Nathan said to David that he had come to inform the king of a great injustice in the land. *A rich man, with many sheep, has stolen one beloved sheep of a poor man and had it slaughtered for a feast* (II Samuel: 12).

Furious at the great injustice, King David declared: *As God lives, the one who has done this deserves death.*

Nathan the prophet responded: *You are that man!*

David was humbled. He said: *I have sinned before God* (Samuel II: 12).

David then took responsibility for his actions. As we have seen up to this point, in the Hebrew Bible, even when others took responsibility for their sins, they were still punished. And so it was with David.

God gave David many wives and many children, but there was great torment and grief in his life. The child he had with his beloved Bathsheba died. One of King David's sons attacked and raped his own sister—another son plotted to overthrow him.

Perhaps after such harsh punishment, G-d decided to forgive David because Bathsheba was blessed with another child—a golden and gifted child named Solomon—destined to be the next King of Israel.

Before we move forward, I want to point out to you that there was another side to David the warrior king. David was a poet whose words became a voice for the Jewish people. He wrote seventy-four of the one hundred fifty psalms that have become a part of the prayers read and beloved to this day. We will delve into his poetry when we move on to the *Writings*.

I have to admit I have a hard time with the way our forefathers lived their lives. I want them to be righteous and honorable and compassionate. Perhaps it is meant to be a reflection of our own lives. Many of us do things we are not proud of, and then we make the decision to take a new direction. This may well be the message in almost all of these biblical stories. I certainly hope so because there is no question that our patriarchs were greatly flawed.

CHAPTER 31

AND SO THE DAYS OF OUR KINGS BEGAN

Book of Prophets: I-II Kings

It is time for a quick review. In the Hebrew Bible, we have covered the Five Books of Moses, and now we are reading about the Prophets. So far, we have taken a look at *Joshua, Judges* (Deborah, Sampson and Samuel), and King David. Now we begin the Book of *I* and *II Kings*.

Solomon the early years

The year is approximately 967 BCE. King David's life was drawing to a close. He told Solomon, the son he had with Bathsheba, that he was to become the next king of Israel.

On his deathbed, King David instructed Solomon on the importance of following G-d's commandments, describing in detail what that required. The king told his son the names of the men Solomon should deal with graciously. He also named those who must be punished: men who had insulted King David. These men were murderers who had shed the blood of war during a time of peace.

After King David's death, we got the specifics on how Solomon took retribution on every man that had been disloyal to his father. When all the enemies of King David had been killed, the Bible says: *Thus the kingdom was secured in Solomon's hands.*

This violence may be difficult for us to understand, but this was considered appropriate behavior in biblical times.

According to the *Midrash*, Solomon was only twelve years old at the time of his father's death. I guess twelve-year-old boys were a whole lot different then than they are today!

Alliances became the young king's next priority. In a quest for peace, Solomon allied himself with the King of Egypt. A pact was made, and Solomon wed the Pharaoh's daughter. Solomon would later build her a palace outside of the city walls, where she lived with his other wives. That is a story in its own right, and it makes for interesting reading and intriguing conversation!

The wisdom of Solomon

Solomon did not ask G-d for wealth or power. Instead, he asked for the ability to distinguish between good and evil and for an understanding mind so that he might fairly judge the Jewish people. Solomon found great favor with G-d, and he was given all that he asked for and more. An example of Solomon's great wisdom is told in the glorious story that follows.

Two women, both claiming to be the mother of the same infant came to Solomon. Solomon's solution: *Fetch me a sword. Cut the live child in two and give half to one and half to the other. (Kings 3:25)*

Solomon threatened to cut the baby in half in order to discover the real mother. The real mother begged for her child's life. The other woman insisted that Solomon cut the baby in half. *When all Israel heard the decision that the king had rendered, they stood in Awe . . . for they saw that he possessed divine wisdom to execute justice* (Kings 3-28).

Under Solomon's rule there was peace and prosperity—the best years in Israel's biblical history.

A geography lesson

Solomon's empire spanned from Egypt in the south to the Euphrates River in the north. His kingdom became the predominant overland trading route that connected Africa and Asia by land. With ports on the Atlantic, the Mediterranean, the Indian Ocean and the Red Sea, Solomon acquired incalculable wealth. It is written that Solomon had forty thousand stalls of horses for his chariots and twelve thousand horsemen.

Construction of the Holy Temple

Now that we have established a bit of a background about Solomon, it is time to turn to his most important accomplishment: construction of The Holy Temple.

Every word written about the construction of the Temple is important because the *exact* specifications of how it was to be built is in the Hebrew Bible, the *Tanakh*.

It is almost impossible to imagine the planning and manpower required to build the Holy Temple. To accomplish such a feat, Solomon had to impose forced labor on all Israel. One hundred and fifty thousand men were sent to work in the quarries and to cut down the cedar and cypress trees in Lebanon. *The Holy Temple was built with only finished stones cut at the quarry so that no hammer or ax or an iron tool was heard in the House while it was being built (I Kings 6:7)*. No hammer or ax or iron tool, think about that for a moment.

In all, the construction took seven years. Solomon also built a palace for himself that took thirteen years to complete. Another great accomplishment during Solomon's reign was the wall constructed around the Holy City in Jerusalem.

Flash forward to present and the Temple Solomon built

In Israel, they have recently excavated a section of that wall south of the Temple Mount. I have toured the excavations. The memories are disjointed snapshots that I want to share with you.

The tunnels smell like damp cement, earthy and ancient. The pathways at some points are very narrow—too narrow when groups tried to pass! I could not help thinking about being trapped underground, terrified one moment, breathless the next, as I realized I was walking in the footsteps of my ancestors.

As we walked along the path, I saw immense carved stones. So immense it was inconceivable to me that they had been finished in the quarry and then transported to the Temple Mount. At one point, we came to an indentation in the wall where religious women were praying. Archeologists and religious scholars believe that when the Temple stood, this was the closest physical location to the Holy of Holies that held the Ten Commandments.

We moved into a cavernous room. I remember climbing stone steps and having the sensation of lost equilibrium, my mind refusing to acclimate with what my eyes were seeing: ritual baths, water pits and water tunnels.

These excavations have given us a bridge connecting us to the history and geography of the Temple Mount from 2,000 years ago. We now know how the Temple Mount was constructed, and I can tell you it was ingenious. The proof: The walls still stand! And the most exciting aspect, the excavations have only just begun.

Too many wives

From the outside, Israel appeared to be the ideal nation that G-d had desired. But again, there was a flaw too great to be overlooked. I previously wrote that even Moses foresaw that there would be kings ruling over Israel. In the Book of *Deuteronomy*, Moses warned that *a king should not have too many horses or too many wives (Duet. 17:17)*.

What are too many wives? We must remember that the mores of the times were very different. According to the *Talmud*, it meant no more than eighteen wives. If that is the case, then Solomon was in big trouble. It is written that Solomon had seven hundred wives and three hundred concubines (although there is controversy that the numbers are overstated). To make matters even worse, many of those marriages were to foreign women—the purpose: to create political alliances.

There is an evocative story about the powerful, ambitious and exotic beauty, the Queen of Sheba. The queen came to Israel to strike a deal with Solomon. She needed access in order to bring merchandise through Israel for distribution to other nations. According to the *Midrash*, what ensued was an illustrious romance between the two rulers.

I have thought long and hard trying to reconcile why Solomon would have taken so many wives. He had to know it was wrong, because he wrote about it unabashedly in *Proverbs*. I am fairly certain you will NOT find this opinion in any commentaries, but here is my take on why Solomon had so many wives. With that many wives, and concubines, Solomon would never be tempted to commit adultery, thereby avoiding the sin of his father, King David and his mother, Bathsheba.

Solomon's great sin

Solomon married non-Jewish women. Yes, they converted before their marriages. But Judaism is clear that the motivation to convert must be born from a sincere desire to join the Jewish people. As outrageous as this may sound, during this time period, it was actually advantageous to become a Jew. Here comes the rub: These women married Solomon for political advantage, and their conversions were not sincere.

Because their conversions were not sincere, Solomon's wives eventually turned toward other gods. And as hard as it is to comprehend, Solomon fell under the influence of these women. While Solomon never turned from the G-d of Israel, he did build shrines for other gods to please his wives. It reminds us again, that in the end, he was just a man: flawed and fragile.

Solomon ruled for forty years but died young at age fifty-two. The punishment for breaking G-d's commandments: Israel would be torn in half under the rule of his son, Rehoboam.

CHAPTER 32

SOLOMON THE LYRICIST

Solomon the poet and writer

We have been introduced to King Solomon, but still we have little insight as to who he really was as a man. It is purported that he wrote the book of *Ecclesiastes* (*Kohelet*) read on *Sukkot*. It is a book that questions life's values. (Biblical scholars, however, contend that The Book of Ecclesiastes was written long after the reign of King Solomon.)

But no one questions that King Solomon composed a thousand songs, or that he wrote a famous anthology of erotic love poetry—*The Song of Songs*. It is often explained that the *Song of Songs* is an allegory (metaphor) for the love between G-d and Israel (Jews).

There are eight chapters to this song and I have picked out just a few of the more evocative lines so you can get the flavor: *Thy lips are like a thread of scarlet, and thy mouth is comely; thy temples are like a pomegranate split open behind thy veil* (4:3).

Thy two breasts are like two fawns that are twins of a gazelle, which feed among the lilies (4:5).

Thy lips, O my bride, drop honey--honey and milk are under thy tongue; and the smell of thy garments is like the smell of Lebanon (4:11).

While some of the writing is almost erotic, there are lines in the *Song of Songs* that have come to symbolize commitment and marriage. *I am my beloved's and my beloved is mine . . .* (6:3) That particular line is recited in many wedding ceremonies of both Jews and Christians.

Solomon and the book of *Proverbs* found in the *Writings*

Solomon went on to write one of the great books of the Jewish people, the Book of *Proverbs (Book of Writings)*. So what is a proverb?

The definition of a proverb according to the Merriam-Webster dictionary: A brief saying that gives advice as to how people should live or that expresses a belief that is generally thought to be true. As an aside, the Bible *Proverbs* are not particularly brief.

I think to understand Solomon; we have to put ourselves in his shoes. As we previously read, King David was punished for his adulterous affair with Bathsheba. Imagine how Solomon must have felt, knowing that his beloved father had seduced his own mother.

An often-repeated theme in Solomon's Book of *Proverbs* is about the sin of adultery. Now we know why. Here is just one example: *Can a man walk on live coals without scorching his feet? It is the same with one who sleeps with his fellow's wife: None who touches her will go unpunished.* (*Proverbs* 7:29)

It also appears that Solomon is trying to warn others not to be led astray by idolatrous foreign women (forbidden women) as he had been by the women that he took as wives.

For the lips of forbidden woman drip honey: Her mouth is smoother than oil: but in the end she is as bitter wormwood, Sharp as a two-edged sword (*Proverbs* 5:3).

When we study the Book of *Proverbs* later in this book, I hope we will obtain the gift of insight into the soul of this great man. And then, G-d willing, perhaps we will even have a glimpse into our own soul.

To summarize the other kings

II Kings tells the story of the destruction of the Temple and the exile of the Jews under the rule of the Babylonian king, Nebuchadnezzar. It is filled with deceit, war, death and desperation, much like the novels so many of us enjoy.

In *II Kings* the northern tribes fled Jerusalem after the death of King Solomon, causing the kingdom to be divided into two parts: Judah and Israel. The next four hundred and fifty years produced twenty-one kings. Sadly, every one of the kings who ruled the ten northern tribes of Israel worshiped idols! If that was not bad enough, half the kings in Jerusalem were idol worshippers as well. Keep in mind that these kings were absolute monarchs, meaning that all the law-making powers were in their hands. Given such enormous authority, it stands to reason, if the king disobeyed the laws of G-d, the people would follow. And most did.

CHAPTER 33

MORE FROM THE BOOK OF PROPHETS

We are now going to meet the men who were granted the gift of prophecy by G-d. Before we begin, I think we should ask ourselves: Why are the prophets important? My take on this question is that G-d needed a way to communicate in words. And so, he chose the prophets as messengers to His people.

Deciding on what prophets to write about was a difficult choice when every single word written in our Bible is considered of utmost significance. In the end, I selected the men who had the greatest impact on the journey I am taking. Those men are Isaiah, Jeremiah and Ezekiel.

The prophets we will *not* be learning about are: Hosea, Joel, Amos, Obadiah, Jonah (yes, this is Jonah and the whale), Micah, Nahum, Habakkuk, Zephaniah and Haggai, Zechariah and Malachi. It is a long list, and I will happily leave these important men for you to discover on your own. So let's begin!

Isaiah

Isaiah was a member of the ruling royal family of Israel. He lived seven hundred years before the Common Era and prophesied through the reign of four kings. During that time, he witnessed the fall of the Northern Kingdom and the growth of a new empire—Assyria.

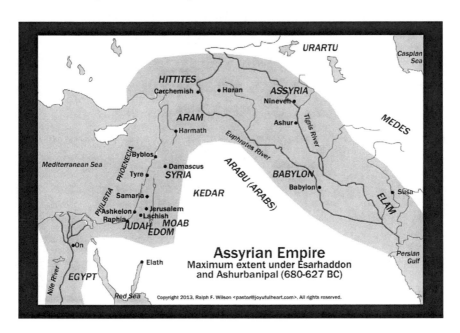

The Assyrian Empire was located north of Israel (today Iraq, Turkey and Egypt). During the life of Isaiah, the Assyrians conquered the Northern Kingdom of Israel (Ten Tribes) and took its citizens into captivity, forcing the Jews to relocate to various Assyrian cities. That left the land of Judah, in the southern region of Israel, isolated and vulnerable.

The Book of *Isaiah* is written like literary poetry. He described G-d's Kingdom on earth, in its last days, in a famous verse you probably are familiar with: *And He shall judge among the nations, and reprimand many people. Then they shall beat their swords into ploughshares, and their spears into pruning-knives: Nation shall not lift up sword against nation, and they shall not learn war anymore* (Isaiah 2:4).

Isaiah tried to instill in the Jewish nation the need for holiness, charity and justice. Unfortunately, Isaiah's messages went mostly unheeded. During his long life, he did manage to instill faith of G-d back into the hearts of many Jews. But sadly, by the end of his life, only Judea remained as the last bastion of a people still believing in One

G-d.

In his book, Isaiah issued dire warnings from G-d: *And when you spread forth your hands I will withdraw My eyes from you; when you speak ever so many prayers, I will not hear; your hands are full of blood. Wash yourselves; make yourselves clean; put away the evil of your deeds from before Mine eyes; cease to do evil; learn to do good; seek for justice; relieve the oppressed; do justice to the orphan; plead for the widow* (Isaiah1:15).

Isaiah foretold of a disastrous destiny where both Jerusalem and the Holy Temple would be destroyed, and the Jews who survived would be sent into exile. Of course, he preached that there was a way to avoid such a horrendous fate: The Jews would simply have to obey G-d's commandments. How many times have we seen this situation play itself out in the Hebrew Bible?

I want to ask you a question, and I ask that you really try to think about it for a moment. If a prophet were alive today, giving us admonitions to heed, would you listen, believe or even consider those warnings? I ask this because I cannot help but wonder why the people would listen or believe Isaiah!

Waiting for the Messiah

The Book of *Isaiah* does have some glorious predictions. Never mind that they don't happen until Chapter fifty-three of his book. In that Chapter there is a poetic song where the prophet Isaiah describes the critical period in world history when the Messiah of the Jewish people would arrive.

The verses emphasize that when the Messiah appears, the world leaders will change their insolent opinions of the Jewish people. It is written that the Jewish people will become the spiritual leaders of humankind.

When I attend my classes with Rabbi Mann from the Chabad of the Venetian Islands, he often speaks of the imminent arrival of our Messiah. It is a longing that filters through all Chabad teachings. (Chabad is an Orthodox Jewish, Hasidic movement known for its outreach to Jews throughout the world.)

This belief feels strange to me: this waiting for the Messiah to appear. I long to believe that one day, the Messiah will appear, and the world will be perfected. At this moment, I am just not sure that I do. What I do know is that I see G-d all around me all the time: in the face of a child, in the sunrise, in the whisper of the breeze and in the diamonds floating on the water every afternoon as the sun reflects its surface.

As for the world leaders changing their insolent opinions of Jews—things don't look very good at the moment. In fact, today I read in the newspaper that the college campuses are crawling with anti-Semitic influences trying to get students to boycott Israeli products.

You have no idea how badly I want to list every Israeli invention that has changed the world! I will control myself and just name two things these students would have to give up: all their computers and mobile phones!

Back to the Book of *Isaiah* and the giant elephant in the room! Chapter fifty-three in the Book of *Isaiah* has become the cornerstone of Christianity. This chapter, in fact, is where Christians lay claim to Jesus as the Messiah.

Judaism advocates that Christianity has mistranslated the original Hebrew text. According to our belief, the words in this chapter, *Suffering*

Servant, in Isaiah 52-53 refers to the nation of Israel. We believe this because in preceding chapters in the book of *Isaiah*, the *Servant Songs* are repeatedly connected to the nation of Israel.

Christians, on the other hand, believe the words *Suffering Servant* is a reference to Jesus. Now that I have put the elephant smack dab into the center of the room; that is exactly where I intend to leave it. The reason: I could write an entire book on this subject. In the end, I am certain neither Jew nor Christian would have a change of heart.

Here is what happened to Isaiah: The King of Judah, Menashe, was so infuriated by Isaiah's depressing predictions that he murdered him! So, who was this King Menashe—killer of our prophet, Isaiah? Would you believe that Menashe was Isaiah's own grandson?

Sometimes, I find myself at a loss for words. This is one of those times. If there is a lesson in this, I do not know what it is.

I will leave the Book of *Isaiah* with this final thought. I pray for G-d to bless all of us and help us embrace our similarities and respect our dissimilarities, as we share our time together on this planet.

CHAPTER 34

THE RETICENT PROPHET

The book of *Jeremiah*

Born into a priestly family, Jeremiah was terrified when he received the gift of prophecy. So fearful in fact, that he resisted at first. Only when G-d reached out to him, did Jeremiah take on the responsibility of sharing his insight with the Jewish people. This took great courage. His prophecies were horrifying.

Jeremiah was born in 655 BCE. During the years of his life, only King Josiah of Judah remained faithful to Judaism. The exiled northern Ten Tribes of Israel were decimated under the rule of the Assyrians. They had become idol worshipers. And the four kings that followed Josiah's reign disregarded the laws of *Torah* as well.

Jeremiah decided to turn his attention toward the northern Tribes of Israel, bringing G-d's words to the Jewish people. Jeremiah reminded the Jews that power and riches had no real value. He taught them that reward came from knowledge of G-d and from following His commandments.

Jeremiah sermonized that *there was no use in relying on man; reward and help came only from G-d.* That last passage is especially important to me. I read it every day in the morning prayers. It serves to remind me that my life and the lives of my loved ones are in G-d's (metaphorical) Hands. Not in my hands!

The book of *Jeremiah* followed a tragic time in the history of Judaism. Under King Nebuchadnezzar, ten thousand Jews were taken captive and forced to live in exile in Babylon (Today, it would be south of Baghdad and Iraq on the Euphrates River.) The royal treasury in Jerusalem was looted and Israel was left destitute. What ensued were deception, murders and treachery. Unfortunately, this is nothing new.

Jeremiah was known as the *Prophet of Doom.* He wrote the Scroll of *Lamentations*, predicting the destruction of the First Temple and the obliteration of Jerusalem. He preached that the Jews must repent and stop worshiping idols and he sermonized against stealing, murder, adultery, swearing falsely, and oppressing the stranger, the orphan and the widow.

Jeremiah warned that the Jews living in Babylon were in mortal danger, predicting that if they continued to assimilate (take in foreign beliefs and culture), they would be absorbed by their conquerors. If that happened, Judaism would cease to exist. The Jews refused to listen, turning instead to false prophets who were making glorious predictions for a wonderful future.

This is not a new refrain. In every generation, the Jews have faced the threat of assimilation. A couple of generations ago in America, it was incredibly rare that a Jew would marry outside the religion. It was considered a *shanda* (a sin). My mother would *never* have dated a gentile, no matter what. Today, many men and women have their prospective spouses convert before marriage. More don't than do.

Desperate to turn the Jews back to One G-d, Jeremiah sent a letter addressed to the Jewish elders and captives in Babylon. That letter became the lifeline for Jewish survival.

The exiled Jews were told to make a home for themselves while in exile. They were to seek peace, build houses and plant gardens. They were to marry and have children and then marry off those children. Jeremiah foretold that after seventy years in Babylon, if the Jews followed G-d's commandments and walked in His ways, they would be brought back from captivity to live again in the Holy Land.

That letter reached far beyond Babylon, and it helped to reignite Jewish faith in One G-d. That message, written so long ago, has been a lasting message for Jews throughout the centuries. Whenever darkness has descended upon our people, we have turned back to that divine message given to us by Jeremiah. Even today, The People of the *Torah* can still hear the echo of Jeremiah's words: *Walk in His ways.*

CHAPTER 35

THE BOOK OF *EZEKIEL*

E zekiel lived at the same time as Jeremiah. He was a scholar forced to live in Babylon when King Nebuchadnezzar banished the Jews from Israel. The book of *Ezekiel* begins with the vision of Ezekiel receiving a prophetic calling from G-d in the fifth year of his exile.

The first twenty-four chapters of this book are about the fall of Jerusalem. I think it is important to point out that all the prophets did more than just foretell the future. They offered a way to change the outcome, if only the Jews would heed the warnings and repent.

Just like Jeremiah, Ezekiel's goal was to keep Judaism alive for the exiled Jews living in Babylon. Regrettably, because of their exile, the Jews believed that G-d had abandoned them.

Ezekiel explained that G-d was indeed punishing the Jews for their sins: idolatry, moral disregard, ceremonial transgression and eating forbidden foods. He warned that they must turn back toward One G-d; if not, then all of Israel would suffer. (I think this just might be the birth of Jewish guilt.)

Ezekiel prophesied the Babylonian army would attack Jerusalem and destroy the Holy Temple. His words went unheeded until thousands of Jews fled the burning city of Jerusalem and poured into Babylon with their tales of horror. Only then was Ezekiel finally seen as a true prophet of G-d.

There is a strange, yet fascinating story, in the book of *Ezekiel: Dry Bones.* The Prophet Ezekiel found himself in a valley, its ground covered in dry bones. He prophesied that the dry bones would be resurrected limb by limb into skeletons and then humans.

Behold, I will open your graves, and cause you to come up out of your graves, and bring you into the land of Israel (Ezekiel 37:12).

The event of the Dry Bones assured the Jews that they would be revived to a new life of glory. Ezekiel prophesized that the Kingdom of Judah, in southern Israel, and the Ten Northern Tribes, living in the north, would one day reconcile and become one nation: the resurrection of Israel (the State of Israel)!

This prophecy served to instill faith and optimism in the Jewish people when he predicted the eventual construction of a Second Holy Temple.

Because of Ezekiel's guidance and encouragement and because he gave the Jews living in exile hope, they embraced their Judaism and constructed synagogues and houses of study in Babylon. Through their actions, these ancient Jews reached out their hands across time and against all odds, kept the light of Judaism alive.

In the final chapters, Ezekiel wrote about Israel's future role in the world. In one of his most famous prophecies, he spoke about the final battle led by Gog, the king of Magog. This conflict would be the final war between good and evil. It would take place in Jerusalem.

The result of this conflict would be the final debacle upon the mountains of the Holy Land. It would be G-d's final reckoning with Israel's enemies and would precede the final redemption: the coming of the Messiah.

And I will rain upon him, and upon his hands, and upon the many peoples that are with him, an overflowing rain, and great hailstones, fire, and brimstone. Thus will I become great, and sanctify myself; and I will be known in the eyes of many nations, and they shall know that I am the LORD (Ezekiel 38:22).

The very idea that there will be a horrific war before the coming of the Messiah is not a comforting thought to me—probably, because in my opinion so much seems so wrong with the world today. As I write this, the presidential election of 2016 is on the horizon, and the country is polarized. ISIS is a threat, not just to Jews and Christians but even to Muslims who don't share their despicable ideology. And in the middle of this tempestuous storm is the tiny country of Israel.

I use to look askance at the Religious Right in America—the evangelical and fundamentalist Christians, but not anymore. And here is why: Israel's survival is as important to these Christians as it is to Jews.

The reason why forty million evangelical Christians care about the State of Israel is their conviction, we are living in the *last days.* They assert that Jews must be ruling and living in the Holy Land in order for Jesus to return.

This fervor originates from the evangelical's belief in the Biblical prophecy taken from the writings of *Ezekiel* that you have just read. Their principles also generate from the writings in the book of *Revelation,* in the New Testament.

The Religious Right may not have the same reasons as I do for wanting the State of Israel to survive, but I don't really care what their motivation is. Israel needs friends, and the Religious Right in America are those friends!

Before we leave the Prophets

Are there people alive today who have the gift of prophecy? Is this an ability all of us have if we could find a way to connect with our spirituality? I know these questions are controversial. I am asking this so that you will keep them in mind as I tell you my next story.

Twenty years ago, my husband and I were walking in downtown Key West on New Year's Day. There was a fortuneteller who had set up a table on the sidewalk. Over the years, we had periodically had our fortunes told. Sometimes it was amazing; other times, not so much. But it was always fun. I did not know then that Jews were not supposed to go to soothsayers.

Before I ever had my fortune told, I always insisted that I only wanted to hear the good things! If they would not promise me that, I would not have the reading. So here we were in Key West, and we sat down with this bearded, hippy-looking man.

I don't remember if this guy read cards, looked at Mel's palm or did nothing. What I do remember is that this man told my husband he was sick, and that he needed to get to a doctor. And by the way, Mel looked very healthy.

It felt as though someone had thrown cold water in our faces! At the time, I can assure you, it did not matter if we believed this guy or not: Our day was ruined!

Mel subsequently went to a doctor. One test led to another, and we found out that he had some clogged arteries in his heart. Divine intervention? Coincidence? Do I think that the man in Key West was our angel? Absolutely. He was an angel who saved my husband's life.

CHAPTER 36

UNLOCKING THE PSALMS

Our learning of the Hebrew Bible is entering its last phase: The *Writings*. Pat yourself on the back. You have come a long way. Allow me to say, *mazel tov*!

The *Writings* include the *Psalms, Proverbs* and *Job, The Song of Songs, Ruth* and *Lamentations*. They continue with Ecclesiastes, *Esther, Daniel, Ezra, Nehemiah, I Chronicles* and *II Chronicles*.

Let's touch lightly over each one.

The book of *Psalms*

Ever since the Psalms (*Tehillim*, meaning praises) were written, they have become the words Jews use to pray to G-d in times of crisis, in times of joy and when seeking forgiveness. In other words, the *Psalms* are our prayers and our sacred poetry.

There is a *Midrash* (story) that tells us King David wrote the one hundred and fifty sacred psalms for himself and for every generation that would follow. Religious Jews believe that regardless of the situation, when you recite the words of *Psalms*, those words will be heard on high.

There is controversy (no surprise) as to whether King David wrote all the psalms. It is said that David collected works from other psalmists and then added them to the ones he composed. Regardless of who wrote them, they were inspired by G-d.

The psalms are hymns filled with praise for G-d's power, goodness, mercy and justice. They are meant to evoke in us a desire for virtue and happiness. The book of *Psalms* is a reflection of the events of our lives, events that occur in every generation: exile, persecution, the desire for happiness, courage and always, hope.

I have a very personal relationship with a number of these Psalms. That relationship has been hard won. For four years, I have been reading Psalms in services every morning. For so long, they did not make sense to me. Then little phrases and passages began to apply to whatever circumstance I happened to be going through at the time: health issues, family situations, world issues. That is why I am excited to share with you some of what I discovered lurking beneath the words.

During our morning services, we read from the Orthodox *ArtScroll Siddur* (prayer book). Even though my synagogue is Conservative, *ArtScroll* will be my point of reference.

I have often wondered where the prayers originated. It was interesting to learn that most are combinations of lines taken from every book in the Hebrew Bible. As an example, one prayer may consist of words from *Psalms, Lamentations* and *Proverbs.*

I will highlight excerpts from the psalms that have impacted me and explain what they mean to *me.* It is important that you understand, these are my interpretations and not necessarily a reflection of what our biblical scholars taught and believed.

At the beginning of every service we read: *Blessed are You, Ha'Shem, our G-d, King of the Universe, Who removes sleep from my eyes and slumber from my eyelids. (Psalm* 136:6) These words remind me to welcome each day as a blessing and to thank G-d for bringing me to this day.

Often times, while I am praying, my mind wanders far afield. I find myself thinking about my children, writing, what I am going to make for dinner and what I have scheduled for the day. But no matter how distracted I am, I always seem to tune back in when we are reading this passage from *Psalm* 136:7: *Have mercy upon us, instill in our hearts to understand and elucidate, to listen, learn, teach, safeguard, perform, and fulfill all the words of Your Torah's teaching with love.*

I have a character flaw: I am not a patient listener. When I have something to say, I want to say it now, partly because I am afraid I will forget what I want to say. So, the words *listen* and *learn* really resonate with me. Once I started writing this book, I found myself going much deeper; praying for G-d to help me *understand* and *elucidate* (explain) and then to *perform* and *fulfill.*

Another prayer that really struck home with me was *Psalm* 34:14: *My G-d, guard my tongue from evil and my lips from speaking deceitfully.* I took this to mean that I should never speak unkindly about anyone. And I should certainly never gossip! How could I live that way? I really thought I would be so boring no one would want to be my friend. In fact, my reputation in the family was; if you told Ellen anything juicy, everyone in the family would know about it before the day was out. Sadly, it was true. I was the first one to share bad news about who might be sick or getting divorced. You get the picture. Although, if I made a promise not to tell anyone, I managed to keep my word most of the time, but not always!

I am proud to say, I have come a long way. I actually try and often manage to guard my tongue from evil.

CHAPTER 37

LEARNING TO PRAY

I have to admit that even today, there are times when I have difficulty with the words I read in the services. So often, they seem out of reach, foreign and confusing. When that happens, I go inside myself and have a private conversation with G-d. When I am able to do that, those are the really good days. I will share with you these special prayers that carry me through my day.

Psalm 30: His anger endures but a moment: Life results from His favor. In the evening one lies down weeping, but with dawn—a cry of Joy!

My father, of blessed memory, had a fabulous philosophy that he lived by and taught me. When I was upset, he always said: *Tomorrow will be a better day.* And you know what? It almost always was. Perhaps, that is why I am such an optimist and why the preceding lines resonated so deeply within me.

I had said in my serenity, 'I will never falter.' You supported my greatness with might; should You but conceal Your face, I would be confounded. To You, Ha'Shem, I would call and to my LORD I would appeal.

This always reminds me that G-d is the reason for every success I have ever had in life. When I am frightened or confused, I remember, I must appeal to G-d for help.

Shacharit

There is one portion of the daily morning service known as *Shacharit*. The prayers are read silently. It is the time when I pray the hardest. I always begin by going through every member of our combined family. I pray for their health. I pray that they will live in a world of peace. If any of them are having a problem, I will ask G-d to help them walk their path with joy and love.

Over the years, friends have given me the names of loved ones who are ill. I have those names typed on an index card: most with their Hebrew name, others in English. When we pray for someone's health, we use their Hebrew name plus their mother's Hebrew name. How beautiful is that? Mothers are the ones that kissed their booboos, and we are the ones who always will.

Every morning during the *Shacharis* service, I pray for the health of each person on my list. Whenever the Torah is read, and the *Misheberach* (prayer for healing) is sung, I read the names aloud to the rabbi.

Let me point out that Jews pray three times a day. *Shacharit* is the morning service. *Mincha* is the afternoon service, and *Ma-ariv* is the evening service.

The Hallelujah *Psalms*

There are a series of psalms in our prayers that all begin with hallelujah. First of all, that was never a word I thought of as Jewish. Rather, I envisioned African Americans singing hallelujah and swaying in ecstasy as they prayed.

I was wrong yet again! The word hallelujah in Hebrew means *praise G-d.* Jews say these praises every day to express our love of G-d.

Psalm 146: *Hallelujah! For it is good to sing to our G-d. . . Do not rely on nobles; nor on a human being, for he holds no salvation. When his spirit departs he returns to his earth, on that day his plans all perish.*

No matter how famous, powerful or connected someone may be, only G-d can rescue us. The adage, *you can't take it with you*, comes to mind. It is what we do in this life that has meaning, not what we acquire.

Ha'Shem loves the righteous. Ha'Shem protects strangers; the orphan and widow He encourages; but the way of the wicked He contorts.

I still have a huge problem with this. I wait daily for G-d to annihilate ISIS and fanatics everywhere. I cannot help but think of the stranger, orphan and widow starving and terrified throughout every war torn country in our world. I used to ask myself: Where is G-d in all this? Where is His help? I now ask myself: Where are G-d's people? Why are we letting this happen?

Psalm 147: He is the Healer of the broken-hearted, and the One Who binds up their sorrows.

When my beloved parents passed away, these words became G-d's promise to me. My broken-heart would heal. That promise has been kept, and along the way, I took both my mother and father into my life in a way I never dreamed possible. I feel their presence every day of my life.

He counts the number of the stars; to all of them He assigns names.

I love this line. When I think of the night sky and the infinite universe, I take great comfort in knowing that G-d has the ability to give a billion stars a name.

Not in the strength of the horse does He desire, and not in the legs of man does He favor. Ha'Shem favors those who fear Him, those who hope for His kindness.

I replace the word *fear* in my mind with the word awe. That is how I hold G-d in my mind: in awe.

Psalm 148: Praise Him. All His angels, praise Him, all his legions.

This psalm then goes on to list all in creation that should praise the LORD: sea giants, mountains and hills, fruit trees, beasts and cattle, crawling things and winged fowl, kings, governments, princes and judges, etc.

I love this! I choose to believe that this is a window into the soul of the universe, instructing us that *everything* has a soul. All that G-d has created has the ability to praise the LORD.

The Bible is filled with verses showing G-d's might, compassion and attention to individual needs. I believe G-d is there for us. We may not understand His ways, but if we believe in His love for us, then no matter what happens, we are protected.

CHAPTER 38

THE BOOK OF *PROVERBS*
A LIFE BETTER LIVED

*P*roverbs is the second book under the *Writings* in our Hebrew Bible. There are only thirty-one chapters in this book. They cover twenty-seven pages when written in English. Solomon is usually attributed as the author, but it appears that others may have contributed. These verses are known as *wisdom literature* and the messages and words are magnificent.

I only wish we could take our time and read each one. Since we can't, we will just get a taste. But hopefully, that will not be enough and you will want to read more. I can tell you that you are really missing something special. It's like taking only one tiny bite from your favorite desert. Yes, you would be thinner, but would you be satisfied?

Throughout the book of *Proverbs* the themes of wisdom and justice resonate. Drifting across the pages are parables and brilliant sayings, each filled with love and kindness, piety and courage. The *Proverbs* are messages that apply even today, sent to us from the distant past, showing us how to conduct our lives and what and whom we should avoid.

Discipline

Fools despise wisdom and discipline (Proverbs 1:7). He who loves discipline loves knowledge (Proverbs 12:1). Sons, heed the discipline of a father; listen and learn discernment (Proverbs 4:1).

For most of my life, I have resisted authority. I think it was one of the reasons I avoided religion: just too many rules. As amazing as it is to me, I find that my mind is slowly changing—the key word being *slowly*. But I am beginning to ask myself questions about why I resist that which can make my life richer and more fulfilled.

I had a rabbi suggest that I might try observing the Sabbath. He said begin by doing it from eight o'clock Friday night to eight o'clock Saturday morning. I tried. In fact I didn't answer the phone, but then again, nobody called. I didn't go to my computer. But I turned lights on and off, and I watched television and changed the channel. The point I am trying to make is that I decided to at least try.

Knowledge

Happy is the man who finds wisdom, the man who attains under-standing. Her (knowledge) value in trade is better than silver, her yield greater than gold (Proverbs 3:13). She (knowledge) is a tree of life to those who grasp her, and whoever holds on to her is happy (Proverbs 3:18).

Jews are seekers of knowledge. And Solomon never let up on the importance of learning—referring to the significance of acquiring knowledge in almost every verse. I like to think that Solomon's prov-erbs helped ignite our desire to study and learn. One thing is certain: Education is an integral piece of the Jewish soul.

Honoring our parents

My son, heed the discipline of your father, and do not forsake the instruction of your mother; for they are a graceful wreath upon your head, a necklace about your throat (Proverbs 1:8). Listen to your father who begot you; do not disdain your mother when she is old. Buy truth and never sell it, and wisdom, discipline, and understanding (Proverbs 23:22).

Take a moment to breathe in those last verses. Imagine if we had made this a daily mantra to our children, feeding it to them with every meal.

Marriage

Find joy in the wife of your youth—a loving doe, a graceful mountain goat. Let her breasts satisfy you at all times; be infatuated with love of her always. Why clasp the bosom of an alien woman (Proverbs 5:18, 19, 20)? Do not lust for her beauty or let her captivate you with her eyes. The last loaf of bread will go for a harlot; a married woman will snare a person of honor (Proverbs 6:25,26).

Solomon warns us to avoid the path of the wicked, and he warns us away from evil women. I have read several scholarly opinions on chapters five and six. They portend that Solomon was warning young men to seek an appropriate wife. I do not disagree, but I contend that Solomon is alluding to his father David's adulterous union with Bathsheba. I think we should also consider that Solomon married alien women who became idol worshipers. So it stands to reason, Solomon was writing about himself as well.

The final chapter in *Proverbs* is an acrostic poem (the first letter of each line is the letter from the Hebrew alphabet). It was written to personify the ideal wife. *She is clothed with strength and splendor. Her mouth is full of wisdom (Proverbs 31:25,26).*

Proverbs 31:10-31 is a poem, known as *Aishet Chayil*—the first words—*a woman of valor.* Friday night Shabbat dinner begins with the singing of *Shalom Aleichem*, followed by singing *Aishet Chayil.* I like to think of this as the husband singing his wife's praises, which, I guess, it really is.

What I understood upon rereading this proverb was that Solomon had shared with us a love story—a story of respect and admiration—something that could only have been written by a man who had known G-d's greatest gift: love.

CHAPTER 39

THE BOOK OF *JOB*
WHEN YOU MESS AROUND WITH
THE ANGEL-ACCUSER

Job was G-d's favorite son. *There is no one like him on earth, a blameless and upright man who fears G-d and shuns evil (Job 1:8).*

One day, the angel-accuser, Satan, came before G-d. (It is important to remember that Satan is under G-d's control.) "*If you take away Job's wealth and his family he will curse You,*" the angel-accuser challenged. I am not going to use the word Satan. I hate it! Remember, I am an unrelenting optimist and I refuse to give evil a name.

G-d gave the angel-accuser permission to test Job's loyalty, as long as Job was not physically harmed. What followed was tragic. The angel-accuser killed Job's livestock, his servants and finally, all of his children! As inconceivable as this is to me, Job's faith in G-d did not even falter.

The angel-accuser refused to give up. With the LORD'S permission, he inflicted Job with a debilitating illness that caused him horrible agony. Even then, Job maintained his belief in the LORD.

Three of Job's friends came to comfort him during his sickness. They sat together on the ground for seven days and seven nights. No one spoke a word. Then in chapter three, everything changed. Job began to curse the day he was born, wishing for death. He cursed his unbearable pain, but still, he did not curse his G-d.

In the book, there is a back and forth discussion between Job and his friends. His friends take the stance that Job was being punished for his sins. Job refused to accept their allegations, insisting that he was a pious man being unjustly punished. In his anguish, despair and perhaps doubt, Job queried G-d: *If I have sinned, what have I done to You, Watcher of Men? Why make of me Your target, and a burden to myself? (Job 7:20)*

Eventually, G-d spoke to Job from the midst of a storm, rebuking him for even attempting to question the ways of the Almighty. Job repented for trying to presume he could ever understand G-d's actions.

The book ends with an epilogue that holds none of the previous rage and pessimism that Job expressed in the middle portion of the book. Job's health was restored. He was given seven sons and three daughters, and all his previous possessions were doubled. He lived to the age of one hundred forty and saw four generations of sons and grandsons.

Reading this, I certainly had to ruminate on the meaning of the messages. The first thing that came to mind was that we most certainly could not presume to understand the Almighty. Bad things do happen to good people. In this story, innocent children and servants died. Yes, Job was given a new family, but how could he ever get over the death of his children? How is this a reflection of Judaism?

Perhaps it all boils down to this: Job was unjustly punished. What is the message in this story? No matter how good someone is, at one point in our lives we will all know great pain, be it physical or emotional. From my own experience, what I know is that with faith, the pain is more bearable.

CHAPTER 40

THE *WRITINGS*
SONG OF SONGS

The *Song of Songs* is one of the Five Scrolls in the Hebrew Bible known as a *Megillot*. The other scrolls of the *Megillah,* (Yiddish: a long drawn out story) are *Esther, Lamentations, Ruth* and *Ecclesiastes.*

I remember as a kid hearing my parents use the phrase in Yiddish, *why are you making such a Gantseh megillah* (a big deal)? I loved that expression, and now, I know where it came from!

I thought the *Song of Songs* would be easy to explain. After all, it is only seven pages long. How wrong I was! I was baffled. Why had erotic poetry about a man and a woman become part of the Hebrew Bible? So, here we go.

In the chapter about Solomon, I quoted a couple of sensuous lines from the *Song of Songs.* I wanted to shock you with the sexually explicit language. I had not really understood what the verses represented.

When reading The *Song of Songs* literally, without looking deeper, it is simply a poem of devotion between a man and woman as they fall in love and marry.

You have captured my heart,
My own, my bride,
You have captured my heart
With one glance of your eyes. (*Song of Songs* 4:9)

Yet, there is so much more than what seemed evident in the verses. The sages taught that the *Song of Songs* was an analogy. It was written to show the love between G-d and Israel. I tried reading these verses using that premise but I found the Talmudic interpretations mind-boggling.

Below is just one instance showing how the rabbis came to the conclusion that the *Song of Songs* was written to show the love between G-d and the Jews. Please note this one was easy to understand compared to many of the others. There is no doubt the rabbis were brilliant, and there is no doubt that I am NOT.

Let him kiss me with the kisses of his mouth. (1:2) Interpretation: *Let him kiss me* was referring to that moment at Sinai when the Jews vowed their dedication to the *Torah*. *With the kisses of his mouth* refers to an angel being sent by G-d to kiss each Israelite.

Let me point out that in the year 100 CE, the *Great Sanhedrin* (supreme council of rabbis) had misgivings about the sacredness of the *Song of Songs*. In fact, there was great controversy about adding these *writings* to the Hebrew Bible. Many found the erotic passages outrageous. The famous Talmudic scholar from the second century, Rabbi Akiva, strongly disagreed, proclaiming the *Song of Songs* the holy of holies. Rabbi Akiva obviously won the argument.

The *Song of Songs* scroll is read in its entirety during the Sabbath of Passover. That seemed so strange to me. Why read erotic poetry during a Jewish holiday?

My beloved spoke thus to me:
Arise, my darling;
My fair one, come away!
For now the winter is past,
The rains are over and gone.
The blossoms have appeared in the land,
The time of pruning has come.
The song of the turtledove
Is heard in our land. (Song of Songs 2:10-12)

We read these verses because the *Song of Song* references spring, and the Passover holiday takes place in springtime. If that was a good enough reason for our sages, then it is a good enough reason for me.

CHAPTER 41

WRITINGS: THE BOOK OF *RUTH*
WE SHOULD ALL HAVE SUCH A
BELOVED MOTHER-IN-LAW

This beautiful epic, *Megillat* Ruth (scroll of Ruth) is read on the holiday of *Shavuot* (More about the holidays later.) I think you will recognize parts of this story.

History

The story of Ruth took place during the time of the Judges, around 1,300 CE. CE, Common Era, are the initials Jews use, and they correspond with AD.

There was a great famine in the kingdom of Judea. Elimelech, a brilliant scholar and one of the wealthiest men in the kingdom, decided to flee the famine in Judea with his wife Naomi and their two sons. His decision to abandon his home was seen as disloyal, casting Elimelech as the man who deserted his people in their time of need.

He took his family to Moab on the eastern shore of the Dead Sea. When his two sons were old enough, they married Moabite women: Orpah and Ruth (daughters of the king of Moab). Orpah and Ruth did not convert to Judaism.

Even if they had wanted to convert, they would not have been welcomed into the congregation of Israel. Conversion was forbidden because when the Jews fled Egypt, they had to fight their way through many lands. The Moabite and the Amonite nations allowed them to pass through in peace, as they should. They were brethren, descendants of Lot: a nephew of Abraham. Their great sin was not offering their kinsmen food or water.

Going home

After living for ten years in the Moabite nation, Elimelech and his sons died, their deaths unexplained. The sons' wives, Orpah and Ruth, were widowed before ever having conceived a child. Naomi was left grieving for her sons and husband. Learning that the famine in Israel was over, Naomi decided to return to her home in Judea. It is important to understand that her decision to return took great courage: Her husband was known as a betrayer of his people.

As Naomi prepared to leave, she urged her Moabite daughters-in-law to remain with their own people. The women refused. They professed their loyalty and willingness to give up their homes and country to accompany their mother-in-law back to the land of the Jews. All I can say is Naomi must have been a remarkable mother-in-law!

Turn back, my daughters! Why should you go with me? Have I any more sons in my body who might be husbands for you? . . . even if I were married tonight and I also bore sons, should you wait for them to grow up? (Ruth 1:11-13)

Okay. This is a bit of a mind bender. In Jewish law, if Naomi had sons, Orpah and Ruth would have been required to marry the brothers of their deceased husbands, even if that meant waiting for them to be born and reach maturity. This was done to insure the continuation of the family name.

Upon hearing Ruth's ominous prediction, Orpah decided not to follow her, weeping as she turned back toward home. Ruth, on the other hand, refused to turn back.

For wherever you go, I will go, wherever you lodge, I will lodge, your people shall be my people, and your G-d my G-d (Ruth 1:16).

The preceding passage is a familiar one. According to the *Midrash*, with those words, Ruth declared her desire to convert to Judaism. But earlier, we learned no Moabite would ever be allowed to convert. Well, I am happy to report that I have unlocked the mystery!

The *Great Sanhedrin*, the high court of the Jewish people, said that the prohibition in the *Torah* against Moabite converts only applied to men. It was the men who had refused to greet the Jews after they had fled Egypt. The women had no obligation toward hospitality; in fact, they were expected to remain at home.

A good man

Naomi and Ruth traveled back to Bethlehem in Judea. No longer wealthy, Ruth went to work as a reaper during the wheat and barley harvest on land owned by a recent widower named Boaz (his name meaning *in whom there is strength*).

Boaz noticed Ruth. He knew she was the Moabite girl who was supporting her mother-in-law, Naomi. He invited Ruth to eat beside him, and he looked after her safety.

When Ruth told Naomi that she had worked in the fields of Boaz, Naomi was ecstatic. *The man is related to us; he is one of our redeeming kinsmen (Ruth 2:20).* Boaz was a relative to her deceased husband. According to Jewish law, redeeming kinsmen are responsible for a relative in need.

When the harvest was completed, and a celebration was to take place on the threshing floor of Boaz's land, Naomi told Ruth to dress up. She instructed Ruth when Boaz finished with the feast and went to sleep she was to lie down at his feet.

When Boaz awakened, he asked who she was, and Ruth replied: *I am your handmaid Ruth. Spread your robe over your handmaid, for you are a redeeming kinsman* (Ruth 3:9).

Boaz was overjoyed when Ruth agreed to marry him, despite his being so much older. Unfortunately, there was another eligible husband with a closer relationship to Ruth's deceased husband.

Boaz offered the property rights of Ruth's family to the eligible man, pointing out that by accepting the property, the man must also accept Ruth as his wife. The nameless redeemer declined, knowing that by combining his property with Ruth's, any son born would have rights to all the property that he owned. Refusing to take Ruth as his wife freed her from any obligation to the eligible man.

Boaz and Ruth were then allowed to marry. The union between Ruth and Boaz produced a son whose name was Obed. Obed became the father of Jesse.

Jesse fathered King David!

This story touched me deeply. It is a reminder that there are no random acts. G-d has a purpose for all that happens in our lives, even if it takes generations to understand why.

CHAPTER 42

WRITINGS: *LAMENTATIONS*
AND YOU THOUGHT YOU HAD TROUBLES!

"When grief pours out" is the definition of lamentation. (And so, I would like to say, *oy vey*.) *Lamentations* are the prophet Jeremiah's dire predictions about the destruction of the First Temple and the obliteration of Jerusalem. Written years before the horrific events of 587 BCE occurred, it is anguish personified. Only five chapters long, *Lamentations*, one of the *Meggilot* scrolls, speaks of the beloved city of Jerusalem and her people in great despair.

Jeremiah was despised for his terrifying visions and for his refusal to remain silent. His revelations resulted in his imprisonment. Embittered, Jeremiah angrily complained about being punished for bringing G-d's prophecy to the Jewish people. Yet, even in his anger, Jeremiah never accused G-d of turning from the Jews. Instead he blamed the Jews for turning away from G-d.

Jeremiah clearly states that the LORD is furious for the sins of the prophets and the wickedness of the priests. They had abandoned G-d and become idol worshipers.

To truly understand *Lamentations*, we need to see the outcome of Jeremiah's prophecy. The Babylonian King, Nebuchadnezzar, fought the Assyrians. He then turned his sights on the Jews. Nebuchadnezzar pillaged the city of Jerusalem and forced tens of thousands of the most educated and prominent Jews into exile in Babylon (Iraq).

The poor and less educated Jews that remained in Jerusalem eventually rebelled. Nebuchadnezzar responded by enacting a crippling siege that lasted thirty long months. There was no food or water; starvation and epidemics ensued and thousands perished. In the final days of the siege, the walls of Jerusalem were destroyed, and the city was set aflame. Millions of Jews died during the ensuing massacre, bringing an end to the empires of King David and King Solomon.

In *Lamentations,* Jeremiah tried to warn the Jewish people that their future would be disastrous. If the Jews had become more pious, would the outcome have been different? Isn't that the real question? How many times have we been warned in our lives? The Jews during Jeremiah's time had the same free will that we enjoy today. Yet, they chose to look away, and everyone was punished. In my heart, I absolutely believe that nothing happens without G-d's decree. But according to our sages, we have free will, and we get to make our own choices. G-d's decree and free choice seem in opposition to me.

I have worked it out in my mind this way: I see my life as a road-map—my path lies ahead. Along the way, I get to make decisions: turn left, turn right or do not turn at all. My destiny, set by G-d, will unfold regardless of my decisions. But, if I make good choices along the way, my life will have joy. If I make bad decisions, I will suffer the consequences. I believe that regardless of those choices, my life is predestined by G-d.

You may not agree with me, but this is what I believe.

CHAPTER 43

THE GLORIOUS WISDOM OF ECCLESIASTES

All the *Writings* in the Hebrew Bible are filled with precious sparks of wisdom. My problem is not where to begin but where to end. With that in mind, I have made an executive decision. We did not study every prophet; therefore, we are not going to delve into every one of the writings. We will learn about the scroll of Esther when we learn about Purim. I will cover Ecclesiastes. As for Daniel, Nehemiah, Ezra, I Chronicles, II Chronicles: I will leave it up to you to delve further.

Ecclesiastes

The *Ecclesiastes* scroll, credited by some to Solomon, is twelve short chapters. It is read on the holiday of *Sukkot*. (There will be more about the holiday later.) In those chapters our sensibilities, vulnerability and complacency are challenged. What follows are my abbreviated and simple conclusions.

We are reminded of all that is constant in our world: sunrise, sunset, the blowing wind and streams that flow to the sea and are never full. We realize that we will never see enough, know enough or hear enough. G-d is always present, and His daily miracles remain constant.

We are challenged to think about what is really important in our lives. The quest for wealth is like spending our lives in pursuit of the wind. And for what: to leave our wealth to someone who did nothing to earn it? Again, we hear the same message in *Ecclesiastes*: G-d knows all and G-d always has a plan.

Perhaps you remember the song by Pete Seeger from the late 1950's, "Turn! Turn! Turn!" (To Everything There is a Season). The song became an international number one hit when The Byrds recorded it in 1965. The words of that song came directly from the scroll of *Ecclesiastes*. It touched me as a teenager, and it touches me still.

> A season is set for everything,
> a time for every experience under heaven:
> A time for being born and a time for dying,
> A time for planting and a time for uprooting the planted;
> A time for slaying and a time for healing,
> A time for tearing down and a time for building up;
> A time for weeping and a time for laughing,
> A time for wailing and a time for dancing;
> A time for throwing stones and a time for gathering stones,
> A time for embracing and a time for shunning embraces,
> A time for seeking and a time for losing,
> A time for keeping and a time for discarding;
> A time for ripping and a time for sewing,
> A time for silence and a time for speaking;
> A time for loving and a time for hating;
> A time for war and a time for peace (Ecclesiastes 3:1-8).

Ecclesiastes teaches us that there is righteousness and justice in the world, but there is also wickedness. There are the oppressed and the oppressors. Some things to remember: We need each other—two people are stronger than one—think before you talk and when you make a vow to G-d, you had better keep it.

We learn that a wealthy man does not always sleep better than a worker. More than once we are told to eat and drink and get pleasure with the numbered days of life that G-d has given to us: Pleasure and joy are gifts from G-d.

We must do all that we can to have a good name and remember words spoken softly by a wise man will be heard sooner than words shouted in furry.

The wisdom of *Ecclesiastes* is a time for us to pause as we ask ourselves what is really important in our lives? We will all experience happiness and sorrow. We will all die. It is how we choose to live that matters.

Joy is what matters. Having someone to hold you, to share with you, to protect you is what matters!

CHAPTER 44

JEWISH HOLIDAYS AND OUR HEBREW CALENDAR

I want to begin with a confession. Except for *Chanukah* and *Passover* I never looked forward to the Jewish holidays. I have spent most of my adult life trying to figure out why. Even now, a lifetime into my life, and after attending synagogue over a thousand times in the last four years, I still find myself restless as the holidays approach.

I could blame it on the fact that I could never get a perfect attendance certificate in school, because every year I was absent for the Jewish holidays. But it can't be the reason because I would never have gotten one anyway! I was the biggest faker in the world and missed school every chance I had.

Over the next few chapters, I will write a short overview of the Jewish holidays. Some will be familiar and others not. Before we begin, I want to share a beautiful story told to me by Boris, a Jewish Russian immigrant.

Boris said that in Russia, they had no Hebrew books, yet their family celebrated every single Jewish holiday, no matter how obscure. They knew all the songs and all the prayers. When I asked him how they knew them he said, "The way Jews always know. It was passed down from generation to generation."

So here we go! Let's begin with a universal rule that applies to all the holidays.

All holidays begin at sundown on the night before the specified date.

Our Jewish day begins at sunset rather than midnight because in *Genesis* Chapter 1 it says: *And there was evening, and there was morning, one day.*

The Jewish calendar

I always wondered why the date of the holiday changed every year. I was fascinated to learn that the date of the specific holiday is always the *same* on the Hebrew calendar. It only changes on the Gregorian calendar—the one most of the western world follows. The Gregorian calendar is based on the solar year and adjusts for the leap year.

The Jewish calendar is primarily lunar, meaning each month begins with the new moon. The Hebrew calendar drifts and loses eleven days every year. This gets complicated, and math is not my strong point. So let me just say that in the fourth century Hillel did astronomical and mathematical calculations and established a fixed calendar based on a nineteen-year cycle.

The Hebrew calendar begins in *Tishrei*, corresponding to the month of September and part of October. The other eleven months are *Cheshvan, Kislev, Tevet, Shevat, Adar I, Adar II, Nissan, Iyar, Sivan, Tammuz, Av* and *Elul*.

Jews are not supposed to work on specific holidays, including Shabbat. *No work* refers to the *Torah's "no manner of work"*. This carries the same restrictions as *Shabbat:* no electricity, no driving, no cell phone, etc. as well as not going to your job.

As we go through the holidays, I will designate which holidays we are supposed to refrain from work. Many of these observances will depend on your religious affiliation.

Jews living outside of Israel celebrate an additional day for the holidays.

We do this because in ancient times the new moon was announced by observation. The *Great Sanhedrin* (High Court) would then declare the new month and send out messengers to tell the people in Israel. Fearful of beginning the holiday on the wrong day, Jews living in the Diaspora (outside of Israel) added an extra day to the holiday just to be certain.

Rosh Hashanah is the exception. Jews everywhere, including Israel, celebrate two days. *Yom Kippur* is only one day because fasting and other holiday restrictions would have been too difficult to observe.

***Yizkor* services (May G-d remember)** A memorial service is held during certain holidays for beloved family members that have passed. At sundown, we light a twenty-four-hour memorial candle.

CHAPTER 45

ROSH HASHANAH (NEW YEAR)

As I complete my book, we are celebrating the year 5776. This number designates the number of years since the world was created. I have to stop here for a moment and address this. In a class with Rabbi Mann, I asked how he could believe that the world was only 5776 years old when they are finding human skulls over a million years old?

He said, "What is the problem? G-d put them there!"

What could I say? Rabbi Mann believes this with all his heart, so I just smiled and thought, G-d bless him.

Rosh Hashanah is one of our holiest holidays. No work is allowed. It begins on the first day of the month of *Tishri*, September on the Gregorian calendar. The translation of *Rosh Hashanah* is *head of the year*. Only, it is not the first month of the Hebrew calendar, and what is really interesting, it is not the only New Year that Jews celebrate.

It is a time for all Jews to take stock of their lives, to contemplate and to remember what we have done right over the past year and what needs improvement. We light candles at sundown on both nights.

Rosh Hashanah is not mentioned in the *Torah* by name. In the Hebrew Bible, this holiday is known as the *day of remembrance* and the *day of sounding the shofar*. The *shofar* is a ram's horn. The most ancient of the wind instruments, it is blown like a trumpet. One hundred notes resound in the synagogue during the daytime on both the first and second days of *Rosh Hashanah*. The exception: The *shofar* is not blown if the holiday falls on *Shabbat*.

There is another lovely tradition known as *Tashlich* (casting off). At the end of the service, on the first day, the congregants walk to a flowing body of water. It can be a creek, a river or in my case, the Atlantic Ocean. After putting small pieces of bread in our pockets, we symbolically empty them and cast the bread into the water. This represents the casting off of our sins. With this ritual act, we usher in the Ten Days of Repentance that occur between *Rosh Hashanah* and *Yom Kippur*.

The *shofar* is blown every morning during these ten days as we pray that G-d will forgive us of our sins. Beginning with the month of Elul, the shofar is blown every morning. As a young child and then as an adult, whenever I heard the *shofar* blown I was sitting among a congregation of hundreds. (These are the two holidays that get the biggest turn out.) I never really felt anything when the *shofar* was blown, just a great admiration for how long the person blowing the ram's horn could hold the notes!

Then everything changed. I was standing right beside the rabbi as he sounded the *shofar* at morning services. Sometimes, there were only four or five of us. The haunting sound went right through me, giving me goose bumps, as I imagined myself walking in the desert, the primal outcry of the *shofar* being carried on the wind. I found it transforming, as if all of our people were being called to awaken, to repent and to return to G-d.

It will come as no surprise that food is an important aspect of every Jewish holiday, with the exception of *Yom Kippur*, when we fast. One of our customs on *Rosh Hashanah* is to dip apple into honey. It symbolizes hope for the New Year to be filled with sweetness. We also eat the traditional bread of all Jews, the *challah*. The difference is that the bread is baked round to symbolize the eternal cycle of life.

We often forget, that *Ashkenazi* Jews from Europe eat very differently than *Sephardic* Jews from Spain and the Middle East.

The *Sephardic* begin their *Rosh Hashanah* meal with a series of symbolic foods: black eyed peas, squash, pomegranate and dates. Their dinner might include roasted chicken, fish and sweet potatoes plus a sweet desert.

Ashkenazi Jews eat things like chicken liver, gefilte fish and chicken soup with matzo balls, brisket, *tzimmes*, sweet *kugel* and strudel. Because I am Ashkenazi, writing this made my mouth water!

When you meet a fellow Jew during this holiday, it is customary to say, *L'shanah Tovah, for a good year.*

CHAPTER 46

YOM KIPPUR

This is the holiest day of the year for a Jew: our day of atonement, the day we are closest to G-d. It is a day when even non-observant Jews will often refrain from work and fast. This is without a doubt our most solemn day. It is also one of our most blissful days. It is a time when we are able to receive G-d's most precious gift—forgiveness.

This holiday appears in the *Torah, Leviticus* 23:26-32. *You shall do no work throughout that day. For it is a Day of Atonement on which expiation (amends) is made on your behalf before the LORD your G-d. Do no work whatever; it is a law for all time, throughout the ages in all your settlements (Leviticus 23:28).*

The *Torah* tells us that we shall not eat or drink from evening to evening as we pray to be forgiven for our sins and to be inscribed in the *Book of Life.* In Judaism, we can atone for the sins between G-d and ourselves. But the sins against others can only be forgiven when we seek reconciliation with that person. This exchange must take place before *Yom Kippur.* Orthodox Jews will not bathe or use any cosmetics or deodorants. Sexual relations are prohibited on *Yom Kippur.*

We light candles at sunset. The evening service for *Yom Kippur* is known as *Kol Nidre,* the prayer that opens this service. It means *all vows between G-d and ourselves.* Sitting in the synagogue during this service is a deeply spiritual experience. In the Conservative and Reform synagogues, a violinist or bassist may play after the *Kol Nidre* prayer. It is a way of connecting with our innermost thoughts. No instruments are ever played in an Orthodox synagogue other than the *shofar.*

Most of the next day is spent in synagogue. The liturgy (worship service) is very extensive. In the Orthodox community, it is customary to wear white to symbolize purity. From my own experience, in the Conservative and Reform synagogues, the women will celebrate the holiday with a glorious fashion show extraordinaire.

The following day, we address our sins by reciting communal confessions, as Jews throughout the world unite in this admission of sin: *For the sin we have sinned before you by . . .* the list is long!

In late afternoon, when we are tired and hungry and our most vulnerable, the *Yizkor* service begins. The Orthodox service is in the morning. It is a time when we recall all the people we have loved and who have passed. Some prayers are said aloud and others in silence. I always cry the kind of tears that make me feel as though my heart is breaking. It is a time when I feel the presence of those people that I have loved: My grandparents, parents, aunts, uncles, cousins and friends. The service ends at sundown with the blowing of the *shofar.*

During the year, whenever I feel overwhelmed in my life, I think of the first two lines of the following poem read on *Yom Kippur* (author unknown). It touches the deepest part of my soul and serves to remind me, yet again, that I have free will in between life and death.

> Birth is a beginning
> And death a destination.
> And life is a journey:
> From childhood to maturity

And youth to age;
From innocence to awareness
And ignorance to knowing;
From foolishness to discretion
And then, perhaps, to wisdom;
From weakness to strength
Or strength to weakness –
And, often, back again;
From health to sickness
And back, we pray, to health again;
From offense to forgiveness,
From loneliness to love,
From joy to gratitude,
From pain to compassion,
And grief to understanding –
From fear to faith;
From defeat to defeat to defeat –
Until, looking backward or ahead,
We see that victory lies
Not at some high place along the way,
But in having made the journey, stage by stage,
A sacred pilgrimage.
Birth is a beginning
And death a destination.
And life is a journey,
A sacred pilgrimage –
To life everlasting. (Author unknown)

The concluding prayers on *Yom Kippur* are known as *Ne'ilah*. It is an hour long, and the ark that holds the *Torah* is left open. The prayers have a tone of desperation as the service draws to an end. The *shofar* will sound and the day will come to a close. Our fate is about to be sealed, or is it?

Repentance, prayer and righteousness avert the severe decree.

It is never too late!

CHAPTER 47

SUKKOT, SHMINI ATZERET AND *SIMCHAT TORAH*

We know how to party!

There is a purpose for every holiday we observe. Some are celebrated joyously and others with a heavy heart. Yet, they all have one thing in common: In order to honor the holiday, we must hit the pause button on our lives.

Sukkot (an eight-day holiday—no work first two days)

Sukkot takes place five days after *Yom Kippur*. It commemorates and celebrates the fall harvest. *Sukkot* is also known as the Holiday of the Tabernacles and the Feast of Booths. It is a Pilgrimage/agricultural holiday as are *Passover* and *Shavuot*. The three pilgrimage holidays, specified in the *Torah*, are the holidays for which the Jews would travel to the Holy Temple in Jerusalem.

This is the only holiday when the *Torah* says: *You shall dwell in booths for seven days, every citizen of Israel shall dwell in booths— in order that your generations shall know that I caused the children of Israel to dwell in booths when I brought them out from the land of Egypt* (*Leviticus* 23:42-43).

The *sukkah* (booth) is an outdoor hut that looks much like the huts lived in by our ancestors when they wandered in the desert for forty years. We are supposed to have our meals inside the *sukkah* during the seven days of the holiday. The VERY observant also sleep in the *sukkah*.

The three walls of the *sukkah* can be built of any material. The open roof is covered loosely with bamboo poles, reeds, corn stalks or evergreen branches. There must always be enough space in the makeshift roof to see the stars—a reminder of the power of G-d as our creator. The *sukkah* is meant to be a flimsy temporary structure, reminding us that all existence is fragile.

Just as a harvest is gathered, we are commanded to gather a *lulav* (date palm frond), three myrtle and two willow branches (*Leviticus* 23:40). These branches are then tied together with strips from a palm frond. Our tradition also requires that we obtain an *etrog*. If you have no idea what an *etrog* is, just as I didn't, let me enlighten you. An *etrog* is a citrus fruit that looks like a large oblong bumpy lemon. Most are grown in Israel, and by the way, a perfect one can cost up to a hundred dollars or more.

What is a perfect *etrog*? One end of the fruit has a stem and the other a *pitam*, the remnants of the part of the flower called a stigma. A perfect *etrog* will be unblemished and have its pitam still intact.

Sukkot is a joyous occasion. During prayers, we hold the *etrog* next to the *lulav* (branches) and shake them. The custom is to shake them in each of the six directions: south, north, east, west, up, down, and then toward our heart. The directions represent kindness, discipline, harmony, connection, perseverance, submission and communication.

The food served on this holiday includes root vegetables, carrots, sweet potatoes, apples and pears. We greet people by saying *Chag Sameach*, may you have a joyous festival.

This holiday pushes me out of my comfort zone—shaking branches. But now, after learning more about *Sukkot*, I have begun to have a different perspective. Yes, the customs may feel a bit strange, but the reason for the holiday is not strange at all. We are thanking G-d for giving us the miraculous gift of food!

Shmini Atzeret and & *Simchat Torah* (no work)

Shmini Atzeret and *Simchat Torah* are both celebrated on the same day in Israel.

Rabbinic literature has a wonderful story about *Shmini Atzeret*. It is pointed out that *Sukkot* is a holiday to be celebrated by all mankind. When *Sukkot* is over, God invites the Jewish people to continue to celebrate for one more day; or two if you live outside of Israel. The rituals are a bit different on the holiday of *Shmini Atzeret*: We do not shake the *lulav* and *etrog*, and when eating in the *sukkah*, no blessings are said.

Simchat Torah (no work)

Simchat Torah means rejoicing in the *Torah*. This holiday celebrates the completion of the annual cycle of reading the weekly *Torah* portions (*parsha*). Let me try and make this clearer. Every week, on Monday and Thursday mornings and on *Shabba*t, we read the weekly *Torah* portion. It is read publicly and aloud in the synagogue in the presence of at least ten Jews. The Orthodox requires ten men. In the Reform and Conservative movements woman count in the minyan.

On *Simchat Torah,* we come to the end of the reading of the *Torah* scroll (*Deuteronomy*). Once the last *parsha* is read, we immediately roll the scroll back to the beginning. The reader then recites the first chapter of *Genesis*. This represents, to the Jew, that the *Torah* is a never-ending cycle of prayer and learning.

In celebration of this momentous occasion of completing the reading of the *Torah*, we pray, sing and dance with the *Torah* scrolls. *Schnaps* (Yiddish word for whiskey) is poured freely and spirits soar!

Chapter 48

CHANUKAH

I spent part of my youth in Rochester, New York. I remember the cold dreary days and the mountainous snow drifts of winter. I also remember sitting at the piano playing and singing my favorite Christmas carols: *Silent Night, Oh Little Town of Bethlehem and the Twelve Days of Christmas.*

Sorry, but *Dreidel, Dreidel, Dreidel* did not make the cut. I never understood why Mr. Irving Berlin, a Jew who wrote *White Christmas,* never wrote a beautiful *Chanukah* song.

When my children were little, we made a huge deal out of *Chanukah,* buying out the toy store. If I am truthful with myself, part of my motivation was for them to never wish they were having Christmas instead of *Chanukah.*

As a child, I loved to look at the beautiful Christmas trees, and I always thought it would be fabulous to decorate one! I had that opportunity as an adult, when a gentile friend invited my husband and me to help trim their tree. Guess what? It was hard work unwrapping all those ornaments! It was pretty when we finished, but I realized I had missed nothing. In fact, as I think about it, every week when I light my Shabbat candles, I get a glow as bright as the lights on any tree.

Channukah (the Festival of Lights) is not in the *Torah* although, the Orthodox will point out many references that allude to the holiday saying it was prophesized. It is celebrated on the 25th day of *Kislev* (December), and as always, it comes out on a different day on the Gregorian calendar every year.

Chanukah is steeped in history, and to understand the holiday we have to get a quick tutorial. Alexander the Great ruled Asia Minor, Syria, Egypt, Babylonia and Persia (336-323 BCE). Jews living under his rule were given religious freedom to pray and worship as they wished. Unfortunately, instead of turning towards Judaism, many of our people assimilated—adopting the language and customs of the sophisticated Greek society. Does that sound familiar?

A hundred years later, Antiochus IV came to power. That is when everything changed for the Jews. Our Holy Temple was turned over to a Hellenistic priest. Jews were prohibited from practicing their religion. The Temple was desecrated: pigs were sacrificed on the altar, and Jews were massacred.

Eventually two very diverse Jewish groups united, the *Chasidim* and the *Hasmoneans* led by Mattathias and his son Judah Maccabee. They mounted a revolt against Greek rule.

The Jews were victorious, and the Holy Temple was rededicated to *Ha'Shem*. In the *Talmud,* we are instructed that the menorah (candelabrum) that stood in the Temple must burn continuously, day and night. Unfortunately, there was only enough oil for one day.

We all know the rest of this story. Miraculously, the oil in the *menorah* burned for eight days. To commemorate this miracle, an eight-day festival was declared. As an aside, we celebrate the miracle of the oil not the military victory. Jews do not celebrate war.

So here is what we do: At sunset, we light candles in a menorah that holds nine candles. The ninth candle (*shamus*, servant) is used to light the other candles. The first night, we light the *shamus,* and it lights the first candle (on the right). We let those candles burn until they go out. On the second night, we light the *shamus,* and it lights two candles, lighting the second candle first, thus left to right, . . . you get the picture. Prayers are said.

Food is a big deal. We eat food fried in oil to commemorate the miracle of oil— never mind clogged arteries! It's a celebration! Sephardim eat fried dough puffs. *Ashkenazi* Jews eat delicious, greasy potato pancakes (latkes). I will forever see my father frying the latkes, oil splattering everywhere. And I will always remember how every bite tasted like love.

CHAPTER 49

TU B'SHEVAT, PURIM, SHAVUOT

TuB'Shevat (work and no synagogue except for daily services, of course)

This is not a holiday or a word that just rolls off the tongue. I would venture to say, if you are not familiar with *TuB'Shevat,* you are not alone. It is not mentioned in the *Torah.*

Let's just jump right in. It is celebrated on the 15ᵗʰ of Shevat (January). The name of the holiday means: "15ᵗʰ of Shevat". It is another harvest holiday celebrating a new year for trees. Remember, I said we have many new-years. This is another one of them! It is a time when the first blooming trees awaken from their winter slumber in Israel and begin their fruit-bearing cycle.

During this holiday, we keep track of the age of our trees. In *Levitivicus* 19:23-25, we are told we may not eat fruit from trees during their first three years. On the fourth year, the fruit is considered holy, and it is given as an offering to G-d. In other words, when a fruit tree is planted, you may not eat its fruit until the fifth year. For Jews, every seed that is planted, and every fruit of the tree, belongs to G-d and is considered holy.

This holiday is important to the agricultural laws in Israel and as it relates to the tithes (a percentage given to charity). Thousands of years ago, before we knew of land conservation and nutrients leaching from the soil, G-d commanded: The seventh year is a Sabbatical year and the land is to lay fallow and rest.

G-d instructed us to allow the soil to rest and rebuild so that it would be filled with nutrients to nourish our bodies. Imagine: We were the first ecologically minded people in the world.

"When you reap the harvest of your land, you shall not reap all the way to the corner of your field, or gather the gleanings of your harvest. You shall not pick your vineyard bare, or gather the fallen fruit of your vineyard; you shall leave them for the poor and the stranger (Leviticus 19:9-11).

This is so beautiful. We are instructed to always leave food for the stranger and the poor. To commemorate the holiday of *TuB'Shevat* we eat carob, grapes, figs, dates, olives and pomegranate seeds.

I want to take a moment to think about trees waking from their winter slumber. I recently drove with my husband from White Plains, New York to Ithaca, New York. It was early November, and when we started out, the iridescent yellows and blood red majestic fall colors dazzled us.

As we headed north, the scenery slowly changed. The leaves had fallen from the trees, the naked branches lonely against a graying sky. I was disappointed and saddened. I wanted more fall foliage. Then something shifted in my mind as I thought about the miracle I was witnessing. These naked trees would soon be accosted by freezing wind, rain and snow. And yet, in springtime, they would once again blossom, bearing new leaves, fruit and flowers. Suddenly, all I saw was the magnificent glory of nature. In that moment, I realized, when we shift our perspective we learn to experience and rejoice in G-d's daily miracles.

Purim (work)

Purim is celebrated on the 14ᵗʰ of Adar (March). On this holiday, we celebrate the survival of the Jewish people in ancient Persia (Iran). We just can't seem to get this country out of our lives!

We learned earlier, that one of the *Meggilot* scrolls is the story of Esther and the story of *Purim*. Interestingly, G-d is not mentioned even once in the *Meggilah* scroll of *Esther*. As with so many of our holidays, we have to dip our toes into the history of our people to understand *Purim*.

In the 4ᵗʰ century BCE, the Persian Empire encompassed one hundred and twenty seven lands all ruled by King Ahasuerus. A tyrannical king who had his wife murdered for disobeying him. The king then held a contest to find his new queen. He sent his officers out to lands to find the most beautiful women in the kingdom and bring them back so he could select his new queen.

Mordechai was raising his cousin Esther, a beautiful orphaned girl. Loved as if she were his own daughter, Mordechai could do nothing to prevent Esther from being taken to King Ahasuerus' harem to take part in the beauty contest. The other contestants, all desiring to be queen, prepared themselves with perfumes, lotions and encircled their eyes with kohl. Esther did nothing. She had no desire to be a queen.

The moment King Ahasuerus saw Esther, he knew she was the one and declared her the Queen of Persia. Under her cousin Mordichai's instructions, Esther did not tell the king she was a Jew.

Haman, a virulent Jew hater, was named prime minister of Persia. (Remember King Saul did not kill Agag as G-d commanded.) Haman was a direct descendent of Agag/Amalekites! Everyone had to bow down whenever Haman appeared. Mordechai bowed only to G-d and refused to bow down to Haman.

Furious with Mordechai, Haman convinced King Ahasuerus (no friend to the Jews) to exterminate every Jew in the kingdom, man, woman and child. Proclamations were sent throughout the land that on the 13th of Adar, all Jews were to die.

For three days the Jews prayed, fasted and repented their sins. They begged G-d to save them. Esther, desperate to save her people, invited the king and Haman to a banquet. It was then that Esther revealed to her husband that she too was a Jew and would have to die. Beloved by the king, the tables were then turned on Haman. He was hanged!

The decree that all Jews were to die could not be revoked, but instead, the Jews were allowed to defend themselves on the 13th of Adar. The Jews armed themselves and rose up against their enemies. On the 14th of Adar, they celebrated their survival. Mordechai was appointed the prime minister of Persia.

Purim is commemorated with a festival. The children dress up in costumes, and we eat, rejoice, give charity and gifts of food. We read the complete *Megillah Scroll of Esther.*

This year, I went to the Chabad to hear the *Meggillah* read. Thank goodness they read the Hebrew really fast, or I might still be there. It was exciting to witness the passion. Every time Haman's name was read, the congregation booed, stamped their feet and shouted in order to blot out his name.

Let's not forget the food. It is customary to bake triangular shaped cookies called *hamentashen.* They are in the shape of Haman's hat to always remind us of his horrendous decree to kill every Jew.

Shavuot (No work)

This holiday takes place on the 6th of *Sivan* (May/June). It is one of the three Biblical pilgrimage festivals that include *Passover* and *Sukkot*. On this day, we celebrate and commemorate the day that G-d gave the *Torah* to the Jewish people assembled at Mt. Sinai, over three thousand three hundred years ago.

The word *Shavuot* means weeks. The holiday occurs seven weeks after the second day of *Passover*. There are forty-nine days between *Passover* and *Shavuot*. It is a time of great expectation. Counting these days is known as *The Counting of the Omer*. Each day, we recite blessings to remind us of the connection between *Passover* (the Exodus) and the giving of the *Torah*.

Observances and rules:

Religious Jews will stay up all night reading and studying *Torah*. It is customary to eat dairy. Some say it is because of G-d's promise to take us to the land of Israel, a land of milk and honey.

Shavuot is the birthday of King David. The book of *Ruth* is read because it records David's ancestry and describes scenes from the harvest festival.

CHAPTER 50

PASSOVER AND TISHA B'AV

Passover: 15-22 of Nissan (April)

*P*assover represents that moment in our history when we became a Jewish nation—Israel. Until that point, we were Jews because we were descendants of Abraham. When G-d gave our people the Ten Commandments and the *Torah*, we united as Israel—the Jewish people. We are commanded by G-d to always celebrate *Passover*.

And this day shall become a memorial for you, and you shall observe it as a festival for the L-RD, for your generations, as an eternal decree shall you observe it. For seven days you shall eat unleavened bread, but on the first day you shall remove the leaven from your homes ... you shall guard the unleavened bread, because on this very day I will take you out of the land of Egypt; you shall observe this day for your generations as an eternal decree (Exodus 12:14-17).

Most of us know the story of *Passover*. We read it every year in the *Haggadah* (Hebrew for legend). I have touched upon some of this earlier. Now, I will complete the story.

Under the protection of Joseph, the Jews lived in relative freedom in the province of Goshen in Egypt. We prospered and our population flourished. When Joseph died, the Egyptians began to see our growing population as a potential threat.

A dangerous pharaoh sat on the throne of Egypt. He enslaved the Jews and then ordered a systematic drowning in the Nile River of all the first-born sons. The shortened version: The infant Moses was pulled from the Nile by one of pharaoh's daughters and adopted by the Egyptian royal family.

Moses did not learn of his true identity as a Jew until he was an adult. Knowing he was a Jew, Moses stepped in when he saw a fellow Hebrew being brutally beaten. Moses killed the slave master. Running for his life, Moses fled to Midian (northwest region of the Sinai Peninsula). He lived there as a humble shepherd for forty years.

G-d commanded eighty-year old Moses to return to Egypt and free the Jewish people from bondage. (Approx. 1200 BCE). With his brother Aaron by his side, Moses obtained an audience with the reigning pharaoh. (No name is mentioned in the Bible.) Moses asked the pharaoh to let his people go. The ruler refused, and that is when G-d unleashed the ten plagues on the Egyptian people. (G-d shielded the Jews.)

The Ten Plagues were: blood, frogs, lice/gnats, wild animals, diseased livestock, boils, thunder/lightning and hail, locusts, darkness and death of the first-born.

The Jews marked their doors with the blood of a slaughtered lamb, and G-d passed over their homes. That is where the name for the holiday of *Passover* originated.

Pharaoh finally agreed to set the Jews free. Once they were on their way, he changed his mind, sending his massive army to stop the Jews from leaving. That is when we have the miracle of the Reed Sea parting—allowing the Jews to flee. (Many people say the Red Sea.)

Observances and rules:

Outside of Israel, the holiday is eight days long. We light candles and say prayers on the first two days and on the last two days we do not work. We are commanded to remove all leavening (*chametz*) from our homes before the holiday begins. This includes bread, crackers, cookies, noodles, corn and anything made from corn like Mazola oil. The Sephardim do eat rice during Passover while the Ashkenazi will not. We do this to remind us that when we fled Egypt, we had no time to allow our bread to rise.

For the observant Jew, the removing of *chametz* is a huge deal. They go into every nook and cranny in their homes to insure that not a crumb remains. On the morning before Passover, we are supposed to remove all the *chametz* from our homes and either burn it or sell the food to a non-Jew until the holiday is over. Then, we buy it back. Obviously, this is a ritual sale.

I put all my *chametz* in a huge black garbage bag and stuff it into a closet. The door will not be opened for the next eight days. That is allowed.

We replace our wheat with Matzo. It is the unleavened bread that G-d gave to the Jews as they wandered in the desert. I love it! What is better than Matzo Brei (Matzo and eggs)? It is not a favorite of some: it can digest like mortar and cause problems in the bathroom department.

For the Orthodox, every dish, glass, utensil and pot is changed (so there are no traces of *chametz*) and replaced with Passover only items.

Seder: The meal on the first two nights of Passover (first night only in Israel)

Seder, we have a communal retelling of the story of our freedom read from a very short book known as the *Haggadah*. There are numerous rituals that we observe before the holiday and during the service. If you have never participated in a *Seder*, I suggest you read further. Right before the holiday *Haggadahs* are available free at most major grocery stores.

For over three thousand years, on the 15th of Nissan, millions of Jews in every nation of the world gather around their *Seder* tables. On that night, we reach back across the centuries reciting the same Hebrew prayers and singing the same Hebrew melodies our forefathers sang. On this night, we are united in our heritage and our commonality. We are the nation of Israel. We are Jews!

Tisha B'Av

Tisha B'Av takes place on the ninth day of the month of Av (August/September). It is no surprise that the scroll of *Lamentations* is read on *Tsha B'Av*, the saddest day of the Jewish calendar. On this holiday, (it seems weird to call it a holiday) we do not celebrate, but instead we go into mourning. We fast from sundown to sundown, eating no food and drinking no water. We omit certain prayers, and we do not wear *Teffilin.*

We mourn and fast on this day because both the First and the Second Temples were destroyed on the exact same day, the ninth of Av, over six hundred and fifty years apart. And sadly, that is not all that happened to our people on that exact same day: In 1290, the Jews were expelled from England. In 1492, the Jews were forced to flee from Spain or face execution.

Chabad teaches that these events are divine confirmation that nothing in the universe is random—G-d has a plan for everything. We have no choice but to accept that G-d's reasons are beyond our comprehension. What we are left with is one very puzzling and complicated concept: *faith.* As silly as this may sound, to this day, my faith is best described in a song. I have whispered the words to myself from the time I was a little girl. I believed every word then, and I believe every word today.

"I Believe"
by Erwin Drake, Irvin Graham, Jimmy Shurl, Al Stillman

I believe for every drop of rain that falls a flower grows.

I believe that somewhere in the darkest night a candle glows.

I believe for everyone who goes astray someone will come to show the way.

I believe, Oh, I believe.

I believe above the storm the smallest prayer, will still be heard.

I believe that someone in that great somewhere hears every word.

Every time I hear a newborn baby cry, or touch a leaf, or see the sky, then I know why I believe.

CHAPTER 51

HOLIDAYS BORN IN THE STATE OF ISRAEL

Yom Ha-Shoah—Holocaust Remembrance Day

This holiday takes place on the 27th of Nisan (April/May). It serves as Israel's memorial day to the six million Jews who were systematically exterminated by the Nazis during World War II. It is also a day when Israel remembers the resistance fighters, those men and women who died valiantly fighting the Nazis.

Yom Ha-Shoah was birthed in 1953 as a national memorial day and a public holiday in Israel. The Prime Minister of Israel, David Ben-Gurion, and the President of Israel, Yizhak Ben-Zvi, signed it into law. There are no religious parameters around this holiday. Yet, some people light a *yahrtzeit* (memorial) candle.

Yom Hazikaron—Memorial Day

Yom Hazikaron is celebrated on the fourth day of Lyar, the day before Israeli Independence day. This is not by accident. These holidays are linked intentionally as a reminder to all Jews that we owe our very existence to the fallen soldiers who have fought and died sacrificing their lives for the survival of the Jewish State of Israel.

At eight o'clock in the evening, a siren sounds in every city, town, kibbutz and village in the country. The siren lasts for one minute. For that one minute, everything stops: even the traffic on the highways. People get out of their cars and stand in silence. At the Western Wall, the Israeli flag is lowered to half-staff.

The next morning (the day of *Yom Hazikaron*) at eleven o'clock, a two-minute siren is sounded, and again everything stops. During the day, an Israeli television station screens the rank, name and date of death for every soldier that died fighting for the security of the State of Israel.

Yom HaAtzma'ut—Israeli Independence Day

Yom HaAtzma'ut is celebrated on the fifth day of Lyar. On this momentous day on May 14, 1948, the Jewish State of Israel was established. In Israel, it is a national holiday and most people do not work.

If you ever saw the movie *Exodus*, then you will remember the scene when Jews took to the streets to celebrate the birth of the State of Israel. Ecstatic and proud they clung to each other singing Israeli songs and dancing Israeli folk dances. Not much has changed since then: The people still take to the streets to dance and sing.

Israelis celebrate by going on picnics and hikes. The holiday concludes with a ceremony known as the Israel Prize. That ceremony recognizes outstanding Israelis for their work in the fields of science, arts and the humanities.

If you have never been to Israel, I pray that one day, you will have the opportunity to go. For me, it is sacred ground. Every moment and every step resounds with the history and determination of our people. I love America, it is my birthplace, but Israel is home to my soul.

CHAPTER 52

THE END IS JUST THE BEGINNING

The journey ends or does it? This just might be the weirdest ending to a book ever. But I still have stuff to share, and I am not ending my book until I do. I call what follows random thoughts. Call it whatever you like. It is a final reveal into my life.

Birthdays

In our family, birthdays have always been a big deal. No matter what, we get together as a family, and we party!! I happen to have my own particular belief about my children and their birthdays. I gave birth to them, and it is just as special a day for me, as it is for them. So I have always encouraged them to spend at least part of their birthday with me. (I am definitely the queen of Jewish guilt. Why not? It works.)

When my mother passed away, and her birthday came around, I refused to pass it off as just another day. I wanted to celebrate her birth. Mom's favorite restaurant was *Joe's Stone Crab* on Miami Beach. (Stop snickering. I go, but I don't eat stone crabs. But my mom loved them!) We go, we eat, and we order a piece of cheesecake with a candle. We sing happy birthday and I cry! Sometimes, one or two of our children will join us, sometimes not. It doesn't matter. What matters is that I feel my mother's presence throughout the entire meal.

When my father passed away, we continued the tradition. Sometimes, we go to Joe's because Dad loved the restaurant too. And sometimes, we have a pool party because nothing made my father happier than being with all of his family. I pray that I will be able to continue to celebrate the birth of my parents until the day that I pass.

Pay it forward

I no longer turn my head away when I see a homeless person! Instead, I make dozens of sandwiches, peanut butter and jelly and bologna with cheese. I wrap them individually and place them in my freezer. When *Chef Boyardee* pop-top cans of spaghetti etc., are on sale, I buy them as well. Every morning, I take out two sandwiches or a sandwich and a can and place each one in a brown paper bag with a napkin and a plastic fork if needed.

Whenever we go out to dinner, I take everyone's leftovers to pass out the next day—knowing that our wasted food is a homeless person's feast. On my way to synagogue, I pass a place where the homeless are allowed to sleep at night. The police make them leave at seven o'clock every morning. I pull up with my car and beep my horn. I hand them food and say G-d bless you. Almost always, I get a smile and the words back: G-d bless you too.

I am not writing about this to give myself accolades. I am telling you in the hope, that you might pay it forward! That is how it began for me. I saw a segment on the news about an eighty-five-year-old making sandwiches, and I said to myself: I can do that too! And so can you!

Illness and healing

When I was thirty-eight years old, I decided it would be fun to try yoga. I arranged for a private lesson in my home. Allowing ego and stupidity to override my good judgment, I threw caution to the wind, trying to mimic every move the teacher did. No big surprise, I hurt myself!

It was weeks before a diagnosis was made: a herniated disk in my neck. I was in so much pain I spent weeks in bed, taking pain pills and kvetching! Over time, my arm started to go numb. It was decided. I needed surgery.

I had my x-rays sent to Massachusetts General Hospital for a second opinion. The doctors at Mass General concurred that I needed surgery. Those doctors also assured me that one of the most qualified surgeons in the country was in Miami: Dr. Frank Eismont, an orthopedic surgeon with the University of Miami. He still practices today, and that is why I am honored to add Doctor Eismont's name to this story.

I checked into Jackson Memorial Hospital, the overcrowded county hospital for Dade County (Miami). It is the teaching arm of the University of Miami Medical School and assuredly, not the hospital of my choice!

As was normal then, I checked in the day before my surgery. All afternoon, interns and residents and anesthesiologists came to see me. At some point during the day, I guess the stress got to me. I came down with the worst headache of my life.

Fighting off nausea and excruciating pain, suddenly, the headache vanished. And at that exact same moment, something astonishing happened: The throbbing pain in my arm and neck also vanished. Excited and confused, I tested my body parts, afraid to believe or admit that I felt better.

In early evening, Doctor Eismont came into the room. "How are you doing?" he asked, his demeanor kind and confident.

I felt tears sting the back of my eyes! "I can't explain what happened, but my arm and my neck don't hurt. Look, I can even turn my head without pain!"

He did a cursory examination and then called my husband out into the hallway.

I didn't hear what the doctor said, but I heard my husband clearly. "Are you kidding? Cancel the surgery? What about her pain?"

They walked back into the room. The doctor looked at me and smiled. "Go home," he said.

Those were his exact words, "Go home." Then he said, "This happens about once a year. We don't know why, but it doesn't really matter, does it?"

I never had pain in my neck again.

For me, it was then, and still remains, an inexplicable healing. I have often wondered why I was chosen. I think, I now have that answer. I was given the gift so that one day, I could share this miracle with you.

Free will and punishment

Is it possible that G-d decreed that hate, greed and evil would unite, and the outcome would be the Holocaust? I find that incomprehensible!

We have free will! Hitler was only one man. Had the world reacted sooner and annihilated Hitler, could we have kept the Holocaust from happening? ISIS! Will we act soon enough, or will there be another Holocaust? Can we blame G-d when we have yet another opportunity and a responsibility to stop this madness?

Will we invoke G-d's rage again? We must take a look around us and try to see with our eyes and our hearts. I am not pointing a finger. I have chased power and money, bigger cars, larger homes and fancier clothes. But, this is an important time in the history of the world. It is up to us to change G-d's decree by making the right choices with our feet, our hands, our voices and our actions.

Why did I write this book?

I had a mantra I said every time I sat down at the computer: *I am writing this book for myself.* I had to say that to still the accusing voices in my head saying: *Who do you think you are? Only scholars write about Judaism.*

My goal was to find a place to begin, and move from that place to the basics of Judaism. I prayed that along the way, I might find answers for some of my questions and doubts.

If I was able to accomplish my goal: to make Judaism more accessible, then I would publish my book.

What have I learned?

Firstly, I have learned that opening myself up, and daring to share my life stories with you has been incredibly cathartic. I never thought I would do that when I began. Actually, I never thought I would do that ever! I have learned a bit about Torah, the Hebrew Bible, our Prophets and our holidays. I learned that there are many different views (opinions) on the exact same subjects. I also learned that sometimes I disagree and have my own interpretations. I call that *Chutzpah!* I realize that the more I know the less I know. But that is okay because I have opened the door and I have walked through.

Where I am today

I still have a lot of questions. I am striving to be a better person: to let go and let G-d be in control of my life. I am grateful for the daily miracles: the sunrise and sunset, the love in my husband's eyes, the touch of a grandchild's hand, the phone call that begins with *"Hi Mom."* I believe G-d and the angels hear my prayers. I pray for *you* and I pray for *me* that this is just the beginning of our journey.

BOOK CLUB QUESTIONS

1. Is there anything you learned about Judaism that surprised you? (Angels, reincarnation, etc.)

2. The journey the author took to learn more about Judaism has had a profound effect on how she lives her life. What might be some of the long term or short-term affects of the book in terms of how you see life and the ways in which you live it?

3. What Jewish customs and traditions do you share with the author? What new traditions did her writing inspire?

4. Which story in the author's life did you most identify with?

5. In the Hebrew Bible G- d is caring and compassionate, vengeful and unforgiving. How do you rationalize this apparent dichotomy?

6. In discussing the kings and rulers in biblical times, what similarities do they seem to have in common with contemporary leaders of today?

7. Do you believe you've had a mystical experience in your life? When? What happened? How did you grow from it?

8. Why would you recommend this book to a friend?

9. How do you celebrate the Jewish holidays? What are your family traditions? Just think; if others adopt your ideas, you will certainly accumulate many angels!

10. What did you agree/disagree with the references to destiny and G-d's will?